Longarm Quilting
WORKBOOK

Basic Skills, Techniques & Motifs
for Modern Longarming

TERESA SILVA

Fons&Porter

Published by Fons & Porter Books, an imprint of F+W Media, Inc., 10151 Carver Road, Suite 200, Blue Ash, Ohio 45242. (800) 289-0963. First Edition.

fw
a content + ecommerce company

www.fwcommunity.com
21 20 19 18 17   5 4 3 2 1

Distributed in Canada by Fraser Direct
100 Armstrong Avenue
Georgetown, ON, Canada L7G 5S4
Tel: (905) 877-4411

Distributed in the U.K. and Europe by
F&W MEDIA INTERNATIONAL
Pynes Hill Court, Pynes Hill, Rydon Lane
Exeter, EX2 5AZ, United Kingdom
Tel: (+44) 1392 797680
E-mail: enquiries@fwmedia.com

SRN: R4137
ISBN-13: 978-1-44024-768-2

EDITORIAL DIRECTOR
Kerry Bogert

EDITOR
Christine Doyle

TECHNICAL EDITOR
ZJ Humbach

ART DIRECTOR & COVER DESIGN
Ashlee Wadeson

INTERIOR DESIGN
Karla Baker

ILLUSTRATOR
Missy Shepler

CONTENTS

FOREWORD

Sewing quilts is my happy place. Designing quilt patterns and creating rulers that make cutting and piecing quilt tops easy for quilters is exciting for me. Adding the binding to a quilt sandwich and hand finishing it is one of my favorite parts of the process because it means I'll have a finished quilt very soon!

A key part of the quilt-finishing process that I found works best for me is collaborating with an outstanding free-motion quilter to add some extra specialness to my quilts. The artistry that it adds to my quilts is unique.

I have learned so much from fellow quilters in local shops, in classes, and in books like this one. The people of the quilting community are what make it special to me. Collaborating with people such as fabric designers, artists, and quilters brings me so much joy.

Especially people like Teresa. When it's time to send a quilt her way for quilting, I'm always excited to see what it's going to look like when it comes home to me. I can always count on a special design and impeccable quality.

I hope this book does for you what Teresa's quilting does for my quilts—adds a level of brilliance to the craft to be enjoyed for years to come.

JULIE HERMAN OF JAYBIRD QUILTS
WWW.JAYBIRDQUILTS.COM

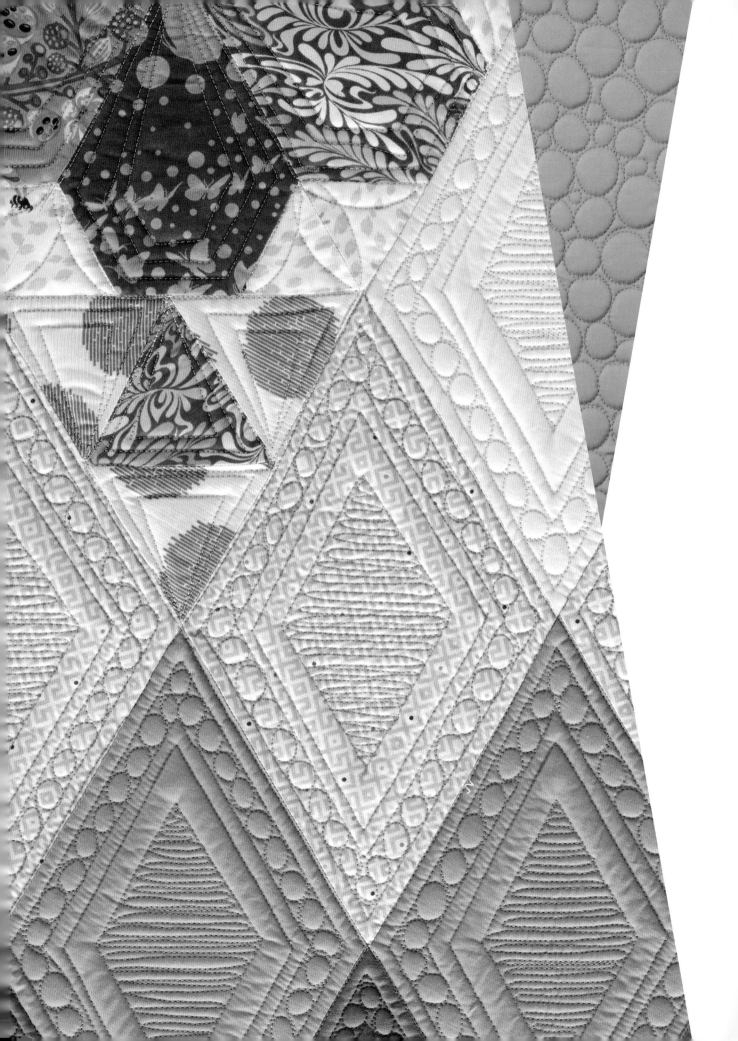

INTRODUCTION

My mother taught me to sew when I was around eight years old. We began with pincushions and went on to sew clothing together. She was an excellent seamstress, but it just wasn't my thing. After I was married, in my twenties, I fell in love with quilting. I had no idea how to make a quilt but was determined to learn. I didn't have much time to take classes because I worked a full-time job, and I had a newborn baby. But that didn't stop me! I bought all the quilt books I could find and taught myself how to quilt. This was before the Internet and YouTube videos, so books were all I had. I became quite good at piecing quilt tops and would quilt some of them on my domestic sewing machine, doing simple lines and allover stippling. Other quilts I'd send out to talented longarm quilters. I always admired the artwork of longarm quilters and secretly wished I could do it, too.

My stack of unfinished quilts grew quicker than I could quilt them. And then, I got a crazy idea: what if I bought a longarm quilting machine? We had the space, and it would help me work through those unfinished quilts. My husband thought I was crazy, but after the shock wore off, he fully supported me in buying my first longarm machine.

I had no idea how to use a longarm machine and hadn't even tried one before I bought mine. But I sincerely believe when it comes to having a passion for something, you can learn anything you set your mind to. I researched as much as I could online and ordered my machine. When it was delivered and set up, my longarm dealer gave me a quick lesson and said, "Have fun." And fun I did have! I loaded up some fabric and practiced designs over and over. I got brave enough to load a few of my own quilt tops, and that went so well that six months later I took in a few customer quilts.

When I started my longarm quilting business, Quilting is My Bliss, six years ago, I was quilting part-time while working a full-time office job. I quilted nights and weekends for many years while I built up my business.

One day, I walked into Stash, a quilt store in Walla Walla, Washington, to show some of my work to owners Kristen McVane, Kathy Hamada, and Ann Hamada. They were so nice to me and encouraged me to keep going. The next week a box of ten quilt tops arrived at my house, sent by these lovely ladies. They said to me, "Do whatever you want on them." I had so much fun practicing and am forever grateful for their support.

It was very challenging at times to manage family, work, and my own business, but I pushed through. Now I'm happy to report I quit my office job and quilt for others full-time. I absolutely love what I do!

All I can say is believe in yourself. If you want to learn something, you can totally do it. Being a self-taught quilter, I have learned by watching others, reading up on new techniques, and teaching myself to do something I love to do. Now I would like to share some of what I learned with all of you. I hope you find this book easy to learn from and master your longarm quilting dreams. It's a fun road to travel based on my own experience. You're likely to meet some wonderful people on the journey. Just remember to practice, practice, practice. You can do anything you set your mind to!

CHAPTER 1
FIRST STEPS

FIRST STEPS

There is so much to consider when you go machine shopping. Which machine will best meet your needs and which features are most requested? How important is dealer support? What size machine should you buy? These are just a few of the topics I cover to get you thinking about your purchase.

Additionally, you'll need some basic supplies to get up and running. Fabric, batting, thread, longarm rulers, and marking tools are essential, but it can be overwhelming to sift through all the choices available today.

You also need to be able to perform basic maintenance on your machine to keep it running smoothly. Sometimes just changing the needle can make all the difference in the world!

In this chapter, I will go over some machine basics and some of my favorite tools to use for longarm quilting. These are my opinions, but I hope it will get you started on your quilting journey and make for a more enjoyable time. Let's get started!

Why Quilt with a Longarm?

To quilt on a domestic sewing machine, you sit at the machine and physically move the pin-basted quilt sandwich around to create designs while the machine remains stationary. This can be a relatively difficult and cumbersome task, especially for larger projects.

While a quilter can become quite proficient at quilting on a domestic sewing machine, I much prefer to quilt on a longarm machine. For me, it's easier to quilt larger quilts, and it provides much more freedom for design.

To quilt on a longarm machine, you stand in front of the machine and guide it over the stationary quilt sandwich. It's like drawing with thread—your longarm machine is your pen and your quilt top is your paper. Essentially, you are just drawing on your quilt top. Fun idea! There also is less strain on your body than when you quilt on a domestic machine. That's because a longarm machine is equipped with wheels that glide freely and allow you to quilt easily.

A secondary benefit of having a longarm machine is you don't need to pin-baste the quilt top, the batting, and the backing together into a quilt sandwich prior to quilting. Instead, you load each layer separately onto the rollers of the quilt frame. The rollers essentially anchor the quilt sandwich so it stays stationary while you manually move the longarm machine to stitch a design.

Not only does this eliminate the need for basting, but it also helps keep the backing nice and flat without wrinkling and bunching as you quilt. This is hard to manage while quilting on a domestic machine. You always have to be aware of the backing.

How It Works

The longarm machine is set on a frame that fits that particular machine. Typically, the frame has three rolls with leaders attached. The leaders are canvas fabric onto which you pin your backing and quilt top. The backing gets loaded first. The backing is attached to the backing roller and to the take-up roller with the wrong side facing up. It's important to make sure your backing fabric is square with straight edges. This keeps the backing straight and smooth while quilting and prevents wrinkles and sagging.

The next step is to layer your batting over the quilt backing you just loaded. Simply lay your batting over the backing for now. Finally, you'll attach the top, following the manufacturer's instructions for the type of longarm machine you have, and machine baste or stitch the top to the other layers. As you quilt and finish the area you're working on, you will continue to roll the quilt onto the quilt take-up roller. Each time you roll the quilt, you will baste or stitch down the area you will be working on. This will keep the edges straight and free from wrinkles as you roll the quilt back and forth to quilt it.

Purchasing a Longarm

When it comes to purchasing a longarm machine, there's a lot to consider. In addition to learning about the features of the machines you're considering, you'll want to be sure you have the dealer support you need for keeping the machine in good working order.

TYPES OF MACHINES

Computerized machines are becoming more and more popular. A computer interfaces with the machine to perform the quilting, similar to computerized embroidery machines. The stitching is precise and eliminates the need for repetitive quilting. The same motif can be duplicated anywhere, such as in multiple blocks.

If you are considering quilting for others, a computerized system is a time-saver. It's much easier to quilt allover designs, also known as pantographs or edge-to-edge designs, than to hand guide the machine, following a pattern with a laser light. You can also do custom quilting via the computerized stitching.

This is a longarm machine that's not set on a frame yet. Once on the frame, the bottom wheels will move the machine for quilting.

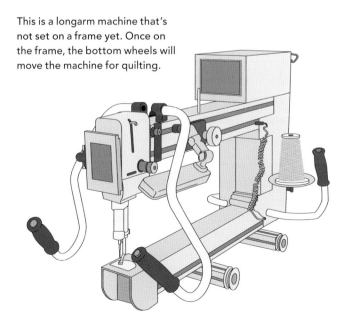

COMMON FEATURES

Stitch Regulation

Stitch regulation is probably the most requested feature on a longarm quilting machine. Stitch regulation provides consistent, even stitches regardless of the quilting speed. Most stitch-regulated machines come with two quilting modes. One mode stops the machine when you stop stitching; the other mode allows the needle to continue stitching so you can precisely turn corners without having long, uneven stitches. I prefer a stitch-regulated machine because I'm very particular about even stitches. It's nice when the stitches have a uniform length no matter how slow or fast I'm quilting.

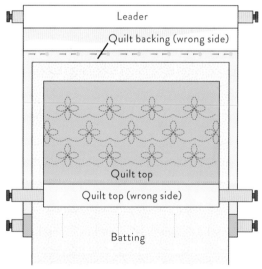

Leader

Quilt backing (wrong side)

Quilt top

Quilt top (wrong side)

Batting

When the quilt is loaded onto the frame, the layers of the quilt are flat and secure.

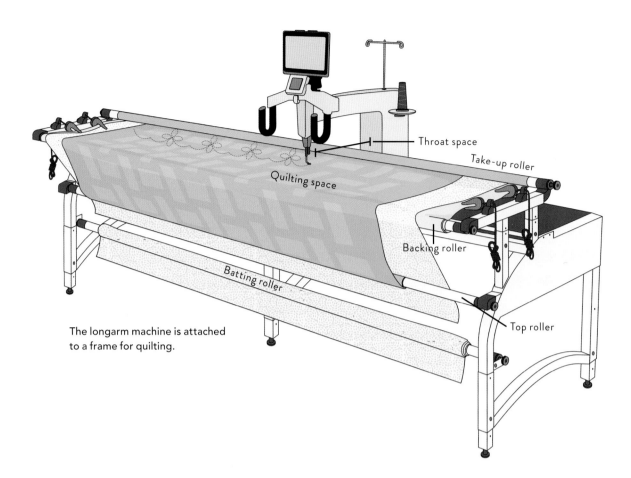

The longarm machine is attached to a frame for quilting.

Throat Space

Longarm machines come in all sizes and with different size throat spaces. The throat is the distance from the needle to the column on the head of the machine, and the space can range from 18" to 30" (45.5 to 76 cm) on a longarm machine. The quilt rolls up in the throat, and the size of the throat determines how deep of an area you can quilt before rolling the quilt.

The quilting space is best defined as the space between the take-up roller and the roller bar. The throat space and the quilting space are not equal and vary between manufacturers, so it's best to research the different brands of longarm machines. While the quilting space is less than the throat space, you want your quilting space to be a comfortable distance for both sight and reach.

It's nice to have a larger throat so you roll your quilt less often. A larger throat also means you can quilt larger designs and work on larger blocks without rolling your quilt. This being said, if you are short, like me, a large throat won't do you any good if you can't reach across the quilting space. So if you have a larger frame, one that is 26" (66 cm), you will gain more stitching area, but you need to make sure you can reach that stitching area. Since I am short, a 22" (56 cm) quilt frame is about as big as I can handle. This gives me about 19" (48.5 cm) of stitching space before I have to roll the quilt.

You can purchase quilt frames in different lengths, from 10' to 14' (3 to 4.3 m). The amount of space you have available in your sewing room will determine what size frame you should buy. Plan on allowing a minimum of 3' (1 m) of space around all sides of the frame for ease of movement while you quilt. A 12' (3.7 m) frame can easily accommodate a king-size quilt top.

OTHER CONSIDERATIONS

Upgradability

If your budget is limited or you want to start slowly, you might be considering a lower-cost machine. If the machine is upgradable, you can add features in the future after you've had time to become comfortable with longarm quilting.

Even if you think you've bought the perfect machine, you never know when you might like to add additional features, such as computerization. If the machine can't be upgraded, you might have to trade it in for a new machine to get the features you want, which will cost more.

Dealer Availability

Does the machine manufacturer have an authorized dealer in your area that will provide you with some basic training and do warranty work on your new machine? Sooner or later, your machine will need maintenance or repairs, and it's nice to have a dealer nearby to minimize downtime. Plus, it's a convenient place to pick up your supplies.

It's very important to have a good working relationship with your longarm dealer. Your dealer is an excellent resource when you have questions and concerns. You want to make sure your dealer will be there for you when that time comes.

MID-ARM MACHINES

A mid-arm or sit-down machine is a hybrid between a longarm and a domestic machine. This system consists of a mid-arm machine mounted to a table that provides a fairly large workspace where you can sit to quilt. These machines are generally less expensive and smaller than a longarm machine, with throat sizes 9" to 18" (23 to 45.5 cm).

The stitching and preparation process is similar to the domestic machine. You push and move the pin-basted quilt sandwich around to create your design, which can put more strain on your body than pushing a longarm machine over the fabric. Mid-arm machines use a foot pedal for your controls, just like a domestic sewing machine, rather than the hand controls of a longarm machine.

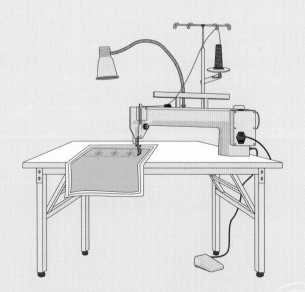

Materials and Supplies

Before you get started quilting, it's important to gather all the right materials and understand your options. There are many rulers, marking tools, battings, and threads available for quilting. I highly suggest you try a variety of each and make a decision of what works well for you.

FABRIC

As a quilter, you are well aware that high-quality quilting cottons are far better to work with than some of the cheaper fabrics you might see out there. It makes the quilting experience so much more enjoyable, and the finished product is of a higher quality. Lower-grade fabrics tend to stretch, can become wavy, and create wrinkles on the backing. The message here is to not skimp on fabric. It pays to use high-quality fabrics.

BATTING

Batting goes between the layers of the quilt—it's the middle of your quilt sandwich. There are so many different styles and types of batting out there. You will need to do some research and find the batting that is right for you; I've listed a few to get you started.

Test a variety of battings to see which you like best.

I highly recommend Quilters Dream Batting. It's my batting of choice, and I love all the quilting options I have with them.

Cotton Batting

Batting made from 100% cotton is very soft and will shrink with the quilting when washed, which gives your quilt a crinkly look. It also breathes well and makes for a nice, soft, comfy quilt. That's why if a quilt is going to be used as a bed quilt or for a baby or child, I always use cotton batting.

Cotton/Polyester Batting

A cotton/polyester batting is usually 70% to 80% cotton and 20% to 30% polyester. It's a little loftier than cotton-only batting and shrinks less than the cotton. This is nice if you want to retain the look of your quilting after you have washed your quilt but still want a nice soft quilt.

Polyester Batting

A polyester batting has a higher loft than a cotton/polyester blend and provides great texture for quilting. I personally love to do my custom work with polyester batting. In addition to texture, it also helps retain your quilting even after you have washed it because there is minimal shrinkage.

Wool Batting

Wool batting is light, is soft, and retains quilting even after washing. It shows the texture of the quilting very well while keeping your quilt cozy and light. It can, however, cause allergic reactions in some people. You definitely want to check with the recipient of the quilt before using wool batting.

Threads come in a variety of thicknesses. I prefer So Fine 50 by Superior Threads because it blends nicely into the fabric.

Bamboo Batting

Bamboo batting is an environmentally friendly choice. It's softer than cotton and is an absorbent fiber with antibacterial qualities. Bamboo is warm in the winter and cool in the summer. It also drapes beautifully and is breathable like cotton.

THREADS

There are so many different types of threads you can use for quilting, and you need so much of it that it can be tempting to go for less expensive options. But my advice is don't skimp on thread! Pick good, quality threads to work with. The quality really makes a difference in your quilting. You will also find that your machine works better with certain types of threads than others. Less thread shredding, thread breakage, and lint buildup are just a few things you'll notice with high-quality thread. Sometimes you just have to try a few to discover which are your favorites.

THREAD TIP

I always use the same color threads on the top and in the bobbin. No matter how great your tension is, especially if you are using dark thread on one side and light thread on the other, you will notice the top thread on the back or the bobbin thread coming up to the top. If the threads blend and your tension is set correctly, you will have better-looking stitches.

The most common types of threads for machine quilting are cotton, polyester, and polyester-wrapped cotton. Cotton thread works well on a longarm, but it tends to create a lot of lint. Just be sure to clean your bobbin area and the bobbin case whenever you change the bobbin to keep your machine running smoothly. Polyester threads are ideal because they create less lint, are strong, and withstand the high power and speed of a longarm machine while quilting. Polyester-wrapped cotton is a hybrid that combines the softness of cotton with the strength of polyester and produces minimal lint.

Thread weight determines the thickness of a thread. Remember that the higher the thread number, the finer the thread. A thicker thread, such as a 40 weight, works well if you want the thread to be the focus of the quilting and not the texture. So Fine 50 by Superior Threads is a polyester-wrapped thread that I use most often. It blends well with the fabric so that the texture shows and not the thread. If your thread does not blend well, it can distract the eye from the quilt piecing.

Remember that it's best to match your threads to the top of the quilt even if you have to change the threads multiple times. It only takes a moment to switch threads, but the end result will be worth it. The more the thread blends, the better the quilting will look. Blending your thread also hides a lot of mistakes, which is especially helpful if you are a beginner.

RULERS

Once you get a feel for your longarm machine, a longarm ruler is a great tool to invest in. Longarm rulers are specifically designed for longarm machines to help make straight lines, curves, circles, ovals—you name it, there is probably a ruler out there for it. A longarm-specific ruler is generally made from ¼" to ⅜" (6 mm to 1 cm) thick acrylic. Regular rulers, like you would use with your rotary cutter, do not work on a longarm. These rulers easily get under the hopping foot, which is similar to a presser foot, and crack in half. The thicker rulers work well with the longarm and tend to not get under the foot as easily. That being said, you need to be very careful when using rulers. They can get under the needle quickly and chip off or even break, which may also break the needle, cause damage to the machine, or even injure you.

For a new longarm quilter, I recommend that you buy several nice straightedge rulers in various sizes. One basic ruler I would suggest you get right away is a 12" to 15" (30.5 to 38 cm) straightedge ruler. You can use it for stitching in the ditch (stitching in the fabric seams) and making geometric shapes. There are many options available. Some have handles to hang on to while quilting. Others are just straight, and you hold them flat with your hand. Give both a try and see what works best for you.

Curved rulers are also very handy to have. You can make fabulous designs just by twisting and turning a curved ruler. Try making curved scallops in a border with a curved ruler, or use it for quilting around curved piecing designs. Circle rulers are great for making medallion designs or circular feather wreaths.

Longarm rulers are invaluable for quilting straight and curved lines. Shown here are QP Edge Straight Rulers from The Quilted Pineapple.

The Mark-B-Gone and Disappearing Ink Marking Pens are my preferences when marking quilts for quilting.

Have fun and play around with the shapes you can create. Some of my best designs have come to me just by drawing shapes on quilts with my longarm rulers. The ideas are endless.

MARKING TOOLS

Quilting designs sometimes require marking registration points or even drawing out a design to follow with your machine. Make sure to use a pen that will come off the quilt easily. I would suggest you test a small area of the quilt and make sure you can get the marks out of the quilt before using.

I recommend using only chalks or water-soluble or air-soluble pens to mark on quilts, and I use only two brands with any quilt. Why? Because I know I can get these inks out with water, and I've never had a problem removing the marks after the quilting is done. The pens are Dritz Disappearing Ink Marking Pen and Dritz Mark-B-Gone Marking Pen. The purple disappearing ink pen lasts for only a short while and will disappear; spritzing the marks with water will also remove them. The blue Mark-B-Gone pen is water-soluble, and it will not go away until you spray with water. This pen is great if you want to mark a design before you load the quilt or if you want to mark a whole-cloth quilt. We will go into this process further in Chapter 3, Doodling and Drawing.

MARKING TIP

Air- and water-soluble ink pens are great to test out your designs without actually stitching them. Draw the designs on the quilt using longarm rulers to see how your design ideas work. It's much easier to spray water to take the marker off than to pick out the stitches.

Troubleshooting

For the best quilting results and a happy machine, it's important to give your machine a quick cleaning and oil after each project. Lint builds up very quickly in the bobbin and tension spring and can cause your tension to be off and make your thread shred while quilting.

If you're having tension issues, remember this: If the top tension is off, there most likely is an issue with your bobbin case. You may have lint buildup or you may need to follow the manufacturer's instructions for your machine and adjust the bobbin tension.

If I'm having thread-shredding issues, the first thing I do is to remove the bobbin case and take the bobbin out of the case. Give the case a quick spray of canned air, or you can just pick out all the lint. A paintbrush works great to clean the bobbin area of the machine, as dust and lint sticks to the brush nicely. Then oil the hook-race area, which is the area your bobbin thread feeds into to make a stitch. The hook race is a moving part and needs to be oiled regularly. Also unthread the machine from the top tension spring and blow out any lint that may have accumulated and then re-thread the machine.

Oiling your machine is one maintenance step you absolutely don't want to neglect. You have to oil the machine regularly due to the high speed of the machine and the numerous moving parts. Without oil, the machine will simply seize up and not work. Make sure to follow manufacturer's recommendations for your particular machine.

It also helps to change out your needle when you start a new quilt. Sometimes if I'm working a large quilt, I will switch out my needle a couple of times. A nice sharp needle works wonders!

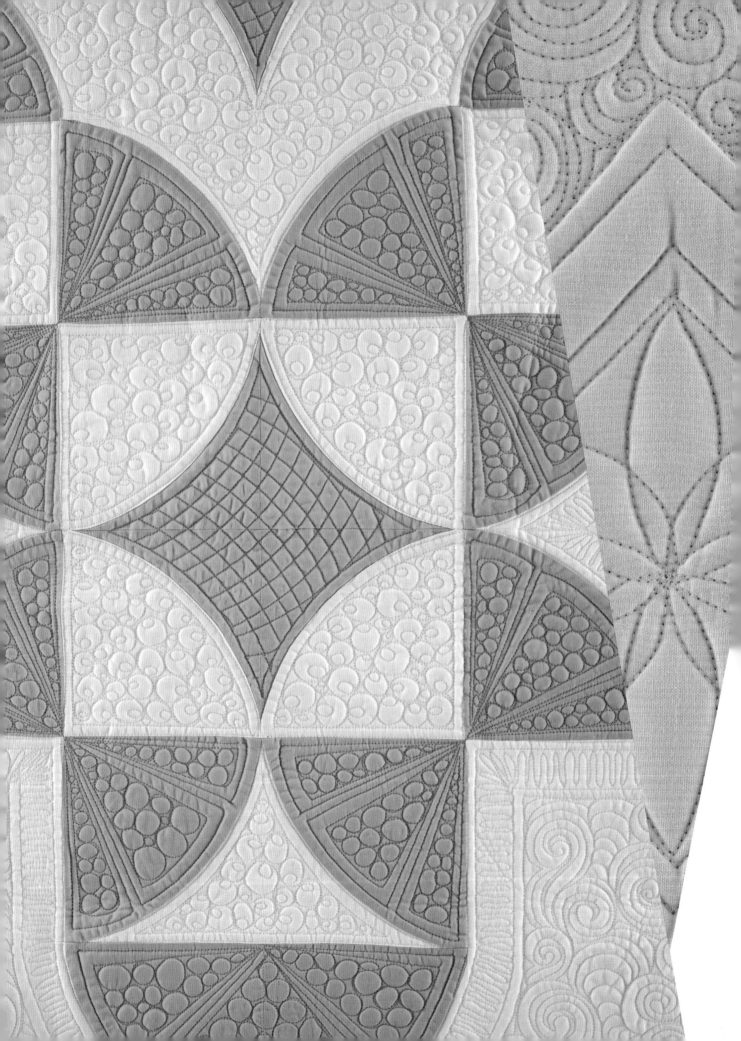

CHAPTER 2
MOTIFS

MOTIFS

There are a few different methods for stitching designs with a longarm machine. As noted in the previous chapter, if you have a computerized machine, you can upload a design and let the machine do the stitching for you. Another method is the old-school way that I learned: using a laser light attached to the machine to follow a paper pattern. Wherever I guided the laser is where the machine would stitch. Both of these are good methods that allow you to get to know your machine.

My favorite way to quilt, however, is freehand. I love the inconsistencies you see with freehand work. And I like that you can customize the stitching to fit pieced blocks perfectly; computerized stitching is very precise and can be almost too precise if the piecing is a bit off.

The motifs in this chapter are some of my favorite designs to freehand. It takes some practice to learn how your machine works and feels as you quilt the motifs. If you find you made a mistake, refrain from jerking the machine back to the design; this creates a messy line. Instead, gently move the machine back on track. Keep it smooth and the design will come out looking great.

Stitch in the Ditch

Stitch in the ditch is the process of stitching in the ditch, or the seam, around blocks and borders. This process requires some practice to achieve accuracy. Stitching around blocks and borders helps them to lie flat without popping up. You can also stitch the entire quilt in the ditch and then go back and fill in with other quilting motifs. This keeps the quilt stabilized as you quilt and prevents puckers and wrinkles in your backing. Use a straightedge longarm ruler for stitching in the ditch.

Echo

Echo quilting is when you follow the shape of a motif or design with evenly spaced lines of quilting. It's great for accenting a motif you have created, and it's a good way to move around the quilt while adding more texture. The echoed lines can be spaced from ¼" to 1" (6 mm to 2.5 cm). I like to echo ¼" away from blocks after I stitch in the ditch. It makes the block design pop, and then I can add dense fillers around the lines while still keeping the blocks highlighted. Echo quilting works great around the edge of feathers and helps to close a design if you want to add some straight-line stitching.

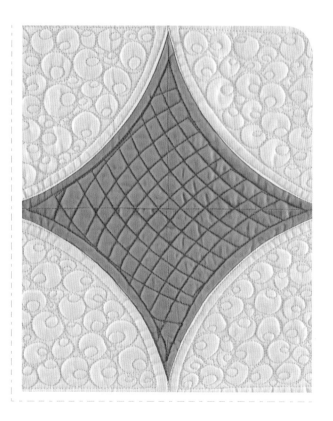

Stipple

A stipple motif works great for quick quilting all over your entire quilt. It also can keep the quilt soft because you can regulate how densely you quilt it. I prefer to quilt a medium-size stipple so it holds the quilt sandwich together nicely after washing. It's perfect if you want to use a cotton batting and get that crinkly look. Stippling can also be done on a very small scale, also known as micro-stippling. Micro-stippling is great to make other motifs, such as feathers, pop or for quilting around appliqué.

1 Start at the left side of your quilt and stitch out a wavy line similar to a puzzle piece. Continue stitching, changing direction and moving across your quilt until you get to the end of your stitching area (**FIGURE 1**).

2 Roll your quilt. Start the stipple at the left side of your quilt and work toward the right, filling in the area. The key to making this design look great is to quilt it so it doesn't look like you quilted it in rows. Make the stipples fit together as you roll the quilt, and no one will know you quilted it in rows (**FIGURE 2**).

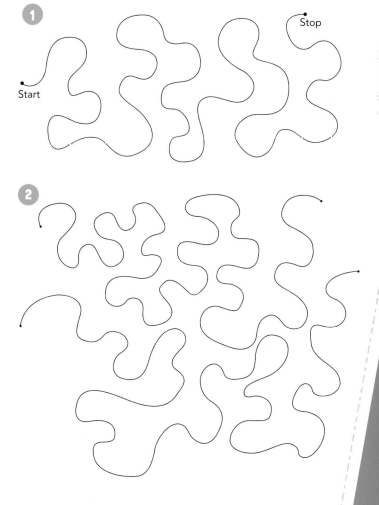

Continuous Line

With continuous-line quilting, quilting the piecing creates the motif. In this particular case, the motif shown is known as Orange Peel.

Continuous-line quilting is great for squares, diamonds, triangles, and even hexagon blocks. Start at one corner and continue around the block. Once you figure out the path, you can easily quilt a large area without starting and stopping. You can also go back and echo around the continuous lines (as shown here) for more dramatic effect.

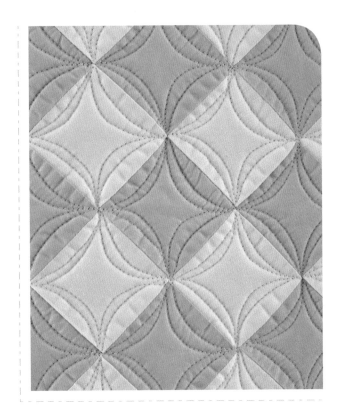

1 Start at the left side of your section of blocks and quilt a curved line touching at the intersection of each block. Continue quilting curved lines down the side of the section and across the bottom of the section (**FIGURE 1**).

2 In the bottom left-hand block, quilt curved lines to the top left corner, then to the top right corner, and down to the bottom right corner. Repeat the same sequence in the block at the bottom center of the section (**FIGURE 2**).

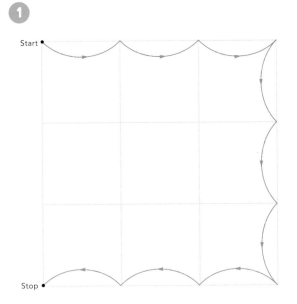

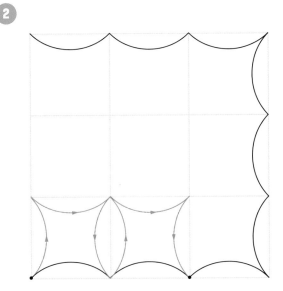

3 Continue to the last block in the row and quilt curved lines along the right side and top. From this point, quilt a curved line along the bottom edge of the right-most block in the row second from the bottom. Then quilt to the top left corner of this block and down the right edge of the block to the left (**FIGURE 3**).

4 Continue moving left in this row, quilting the bottoms and sides of each block (shown in dark gray). Quilt the top curves of the blocks in this row, moving from left to right (shown in medium gray). Quilt the bottoms and sides of the blocks in the top row up, again moving from right to left (shown in light gray dashed). You'll finish the section in the top left corner, where you began (**FIGURE 4**).

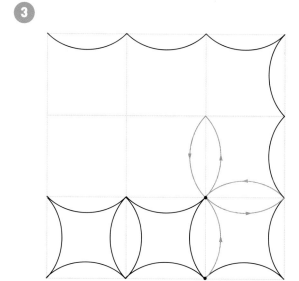

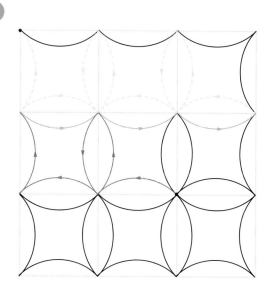

Loops

Loops are a simple motif that can be quilted quickly. Loops work great as an allover motif for an entire quilt or as a filler motif.

1 Make a curved line with a circle at the end (**FIGURE 1**).

2 Curve out of the circle design and make another circle on the end. Continue to twist and turn, filling in the area where you are working (**FIGURE 2**).

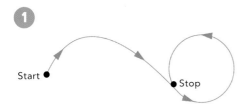

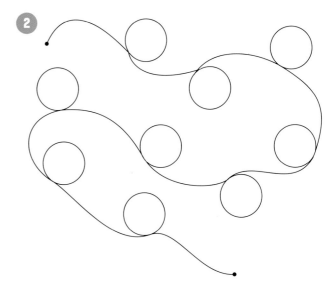

Ls and Es

This motif is simply quilting lowercase Ls and Es. Crazy, huh? The motif is very simple to quilt and works great in borders and sashing. I like to use it when I don't want the quilting to be very dense.

1 Quilt a lowercase L (**FIGURE 1**).

2 Loop out of the L and make a lowercase E (**FIGURE 2**).

3 Continue along until the end of your space. If quilting a border, curve the shape in the corners (**FIGURE 3**).

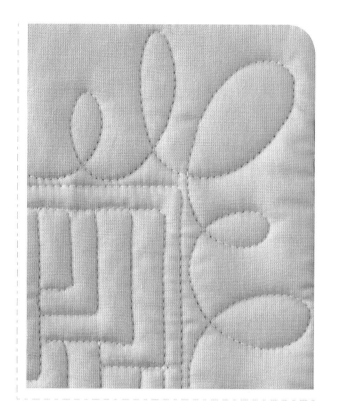

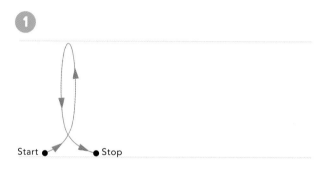

Start • Stop

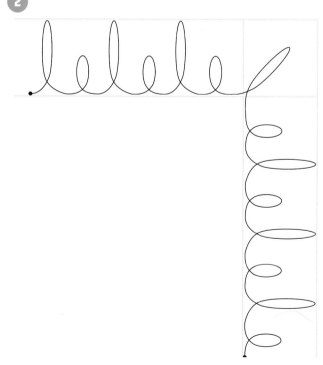

Up-and-Around Background

This design is fun to use as a background filler. It also works as a good filler around appliqué blocks.

1 Quilt a vertical up-down curvy shape. I like to make 2 humps to start and then come back up and stop about ¼" (6 mm) away from the top of the adjacent hump (**FIGURE 1**).

2 Change direction and quilt the curvy shapes horizontally (**FIGURE 2**).

3 Continue making this shape, alternating directions, to fill the background space. Try to keep the rows as straight as you can and keep your spacing consistent (**FIGURE 3**).

4 To do a larger area, stitch down and quilt the next row in the opposite direction. Repeat as needed to fill the entire area or even the entire quilt (**FIGURE 4**).

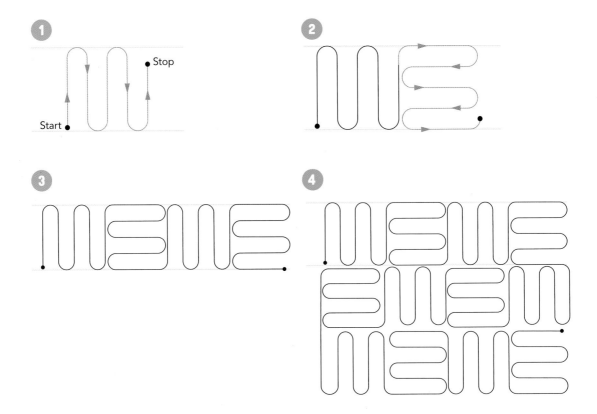

Water

The water motif is great to use on landscape quilts where water, sand, or even gravel is depicted. It gives some depth to the space you are filling.

1 Quilt a curved line and curve to the left then back to the right (**FIGURE 1**).

2 Continue to create back-and-forth lines going horizontally left to right, varying the width of the curve (**FIGURE 2**).

3 Keep making back-and-forth curves, alternating directions, and fill in areas to create the depth of the design (**FIGURE 3**).

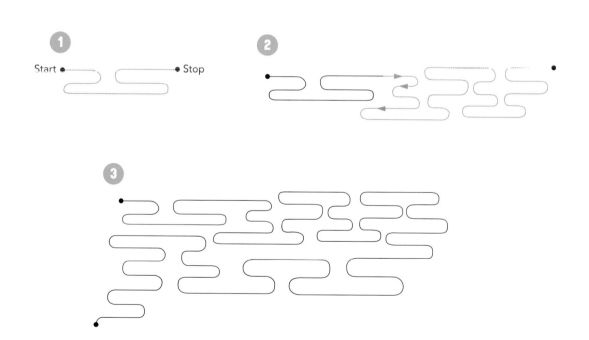

Wishbones, or Figure 8s

Wishbones are very versatile and work well in borders and also as a background filler. You can quilt wishbones close together or space them apart to keep the quilting softer.

1 Start at the top left corner of your space and stitch an almost straight line with a curve at the tip that touches the bottom of the space. Stitch upward, crossing over the downward line (**FIGURE 1**).

2 Continue upward and make a curve at the top of the space (**FIGURE 2**).

3 Continue alternating the loops all along the space (**FIGURE 3**).

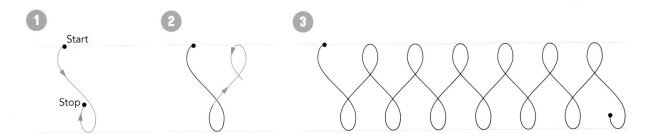

ZIGZAG IT

Try quilting this design in a zigzag pattern or in shapes such as triangles, squares, or diamonds. Wishbones adapt well to most shapes.

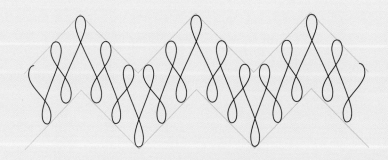

Swirls

Swirls are a basic modern motif that you see on lots of quilts. Swirls offer a fresh approach to filling negative quilting space with visual movement. There are a couple different styles of swirls that can change the look of the motif. You may find that once you start making swirls, you'll come up with your own style and look. Here are three swirl motifs to get you started.

BASIC SWIRLS

Basic swirls are an easy way to fill in an area, and I absolutely love the look of them. You quilt into the spiral, leaving enough space to spiral back out. Then backtrack a little to get to the next starting spot. Spiral in and then spiral back out as the drawing demonstrates. You will notice the spirals look like they are coming out from one another or stacking on top of each other. The spacing within and between basic swirls is usually even, which takes a bit of practice. Use your hopping foot as a spacing guide. Once you get the hang of it, swirls go quite quickly.

1 Quilt a swirl shape, leaving space to swirl back out of the motif. The trick is to keep the spacing even. Swirl back out, making sure to swirl back to where you started (**FIGURE 1**).

2 Backtrack up to the space where you want to start a new swirl. Quilt another swirl shape, but this time change the direction so the spirals are not going the same direction. Make sure to swirl back out to where you started this second swirl (**FIGURE 2**).

3 Continue to travel along your quilt top, adding more swirls and making sure to change directions to create movement. If you get in a corner, just backtrack along another swirl to get where you need to be (**FIGURE 3**).

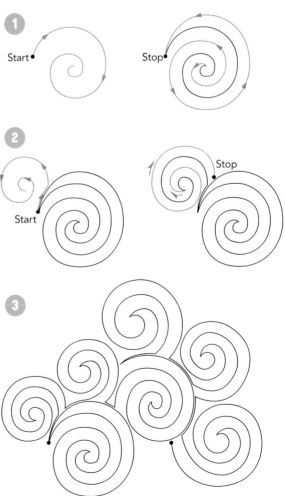

ALTERNATING SWIRL BORDER

The alternating swirl border motif is very modern and is a great way to fill borders 2" to 3" (5 to 7.5 cm) wide. If you make the motif bigger than that, it gets a little wonky looking.

1 Quilt a basic swirl. Swirl out of the swirl and stop at the top of the swirl (**FIGURE 1**).

2 Travel down the curve. Stitch the next swirl in the opposite direction of the first swirl (**FIGURE 2**).

3 Continue alternating swirls until you reach the end of your border (**FIGURE 3**).

4 At the corner, continue to make this same motif going down instead of across (**FIGURE 4**).

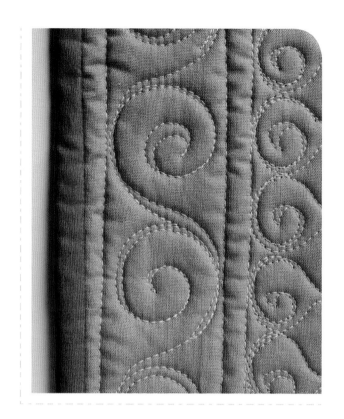

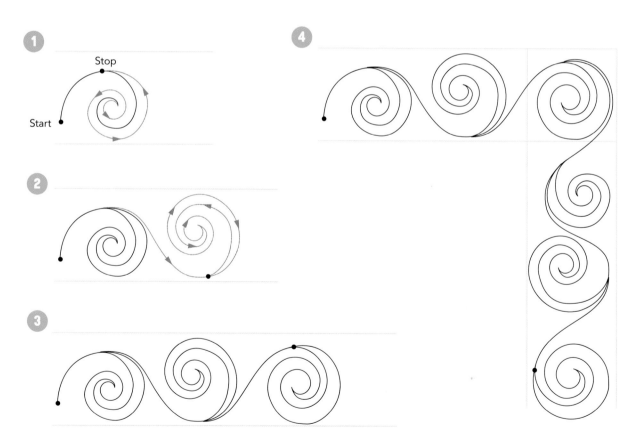

SWIRLS WITH TAILS

These swirls are made the same way as the basic swirls except you make a long flowing tail as you come out of the swirl and then swirl back in. These are fun to mix with basic swirls because they give a lot of movement. Use this motif if you're trying to get the appearance of wind or waves.

1 Quilt a long curvy line and add a swirl to the end of it. Make sure you leave enough room to swirl back out of this shape (**FIGURE 1**).

2 Swirl back out of the shape, following the shape back to the starting point. Taper the end off like a tail (**FIGURE 2**).

3 From this point, follow the top of the shape into the swirl and continue the swirl on the outside all the way back down to your starting position on the tail. It sounds complicated, but you are simply echoing the footprint of the swirl (**FIGURE 3**).

4 Build on this design by mixing some basic swirls with the swirl tails. Remember to change the direction of the swirls to keep them flowing nicely (**FIGURE 4**).

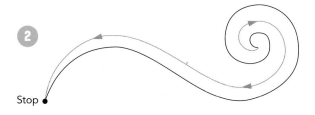

Pebbles

Pebbles are a very forgiving motif and work great for fillers around appliqué or in large areas of negative space to create beautiful texture. The wonderful thing about pebbles is that they are very versatile. You can add them to other motifs, or you can vary the size and scale of the pebbles for a different look.

1 Begin making a circle clockwise (**FIGURE 1**).

2 Make a circle counterclockwise, away from the first circle you just made (**FIGURE 2**).

3 Make another clockwise circle and continue to fill in the space alternating between clockwise and counterclockwise circles. If you get stuck in an area, simply follow the existing quilting to get to the next area (**FIGURE 3**).

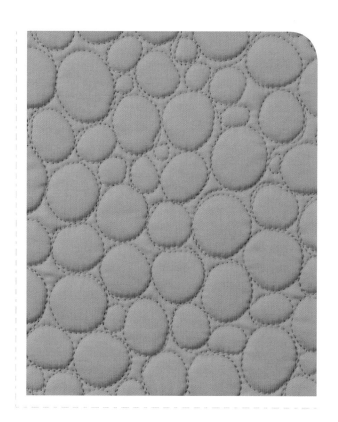

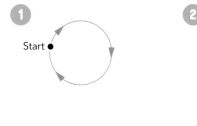

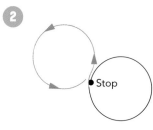

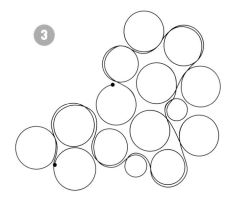

PEBBLES AND SWIRLS

Give the pebbles a unique look by mixing them with some swirls with tails. These motifs work great together and make it easy to go from one motif to the other while providing some really awesome texture.

Double Bubbles

Double bubbles are a variation of a simple pebble and have a very dense, dramatic look. This filler works great around other motifs such as swirls, feathers, clamshells, and paisleys.

1 Start by quilting a circle or pebble in a clockwise direction (**FIGURE 1**).

2 Quilt another smaller clockwise circle inside the first circle. You now have a circle within a circle (**FIGURE 2**).

3 Quilt another large circle in the opposite direction you just quilted (counterclockwise) (**FIGURE 3**).

4 Quilt a smaller circle counterclockwise inside the larger circle you just quilted (**FIGURE 4**).

5 Continue to make double bubbles, alternating directions. Again, if you get stuck in an area, follow the existing quilting to a new area (**FIGURE 5**).

Quilt your double bubbles close together to make the motif dense. Or make the double bubbles a little larger to keep the motif soft.

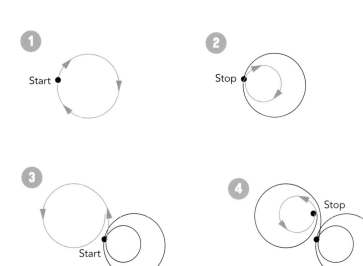

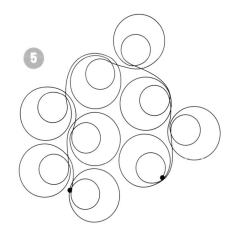

Paisleys

Paisleys are fun fillers for any time, but they work especially well with feathers. That's because paisleys are very easy to curve into small areas. They work great when you twist and turn them to create movement and texture. You can make big or small paisleys and can change the look just by changing the scale of the motif.

1 Start at the pointed tip at the base of the motif and quilt a paisley shape, leaving enough space to create another paisley inside the first one. The paisley is basically a large loop that curves back and narrows to create a pointed tip where you started (**FIGURE 1**).

2 Quilt a smaller paisley inside the larger paisley you just quilted. Make sure to keep the spacing even. You have just created a complete paisley (**FIGURE 2**).

3 Make another paisley next to the first paisley (**FIGURE 3**).

4 Fill in the space with more paisleys that twist and turn in opposite directions. By doing this, you create movement in the quilting (**FIGURE 4**).

5 If you get in a tight corner, just backtrack out of the area and continue quilting in a new area (**FIGURE 5**).

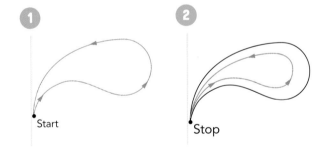

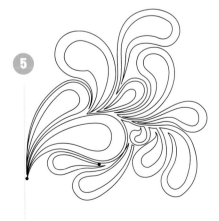

Clamshells

Clamshells are very similar to paisleys except they are not as curved or elongated. You make a curved shape and echo out of the shape like you would a paisley. Clamshells are a simple and fast motif to quilt. They are also great to fill in large areas quickly while providing texture. Clamshells are easy to echo around, and you can easily move to other areas without starting and stopping.

1 Make a small seedlike shape, returning to where you started (**FIGURE 1**).

2 Echo this shape around the outside in the opposite direction so that one clamshell is inside the other (**FIGURE 2**).

3 Make another small seedlike shape next to the first one and echo it. Sometimes I will echo 3 or 4 times. The additional echoes just give more texture (**FIGURE 3**).

4 Continue to make new seedlike shapes and echo them to fill the quilting area. If you get stuck, just echo out of that shape another time or two to get where you need to be (**FIGURE 4**).

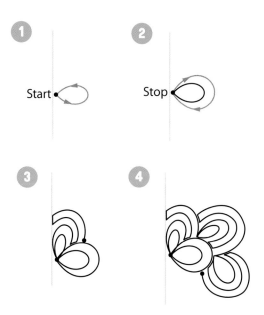

MAKE PRACTICE PRETTY

As you'll see in Chapter 3, Doodling and Drawing, one great way to practice is to load a simple quilt sandwich. Load backing fabric, layer batting, and use a solid fabric for the top. Use a matching thread to help hide mistakes. Try out different motifs, filling the whole fabric. The result will be a beautiful tone-on-tone look. Make it a rectangular shape, and you will have a lovely table runner when it's complete. It's a great way to practice!

Ribbon Candy

Ribbon candy is one of my favorite designs to quilt. Ribbon candy is very simple but can be used in lots of spaces, including borders and sashing.

1 Start at the top left corner of your space. Make a curved shape almost like a backward S until you hit the bottom of your space (**FIGURE 1**).

2 Continue to curve up to the top of the border, making a front-facing S. Try not to cross over when the 2 curves meet (**FIGURE 2**).

3 Continue along your space until you reach the end (**FIGURE 3**).

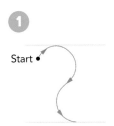

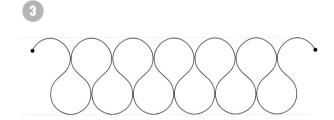

BORDER TREATMENT

When stitching a border, I like to stitch the ribbon candy through the end of the border and complete the motif at the end of the corner. Then I travel down to the next border. I prefer to do it this way rather than curving the motif into the corner and around to the next border. The curved motif makes the shape of the corner seem distorted to me.

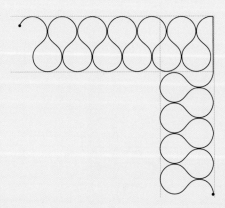

RIBBON CANDY VARIATION

You can change the look of the ribbon candy motif just by echoing both sides of the ribbon.

1 Make your ribbon candy as previously described but space the loops out a bit to allow for echoing on both sides of the ribbon (**FIGURE 1**).

2 After the first pass of ribbon candy, echo quilt in one direction as shown (**FIGURE 2**).

3 Echo the other side of your ribbon candy on the third pass, and the motif is now complete (**FIGURE 3**).

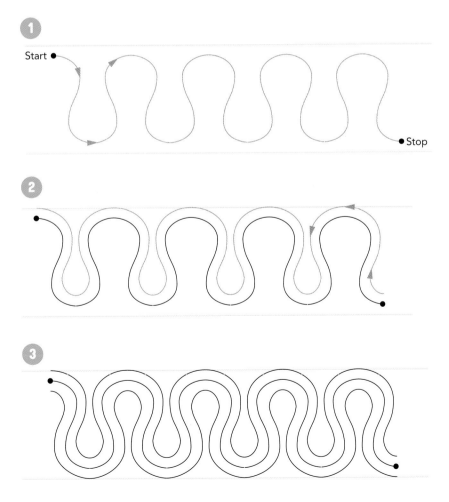

① Start ● ● Stop

②

③

SWIRL RIBBON CANDY

Swirl ribbon candy works well in borders and looks a little fancier than the traditional ribbon candy design.

1 Quilt a curved backward S, the same way you start basic ribbon candy (**FIGURE 1**).

2 Curve around and make a swirl at the bottom (**FIGURE 2**).

3 Swirl back out of the swirl and curve up into a forward-facing S (**FIGURE 3**).

4 Continue down to make another backward S. Backtrack along this S until you are level with the top of the swirl shape at the bottom of the adjacent S. Make a small loop design inside the ribbon candy and travel down to the bottom of the S (**FIGURE 4**).

5 Make another swirl at the bottom of the backward S like you did in Steps 2 and 3 (**FIGURE 5**).

6 Continue making swirled ribbon candy shapes along the entire space (**FIGURE 6**).

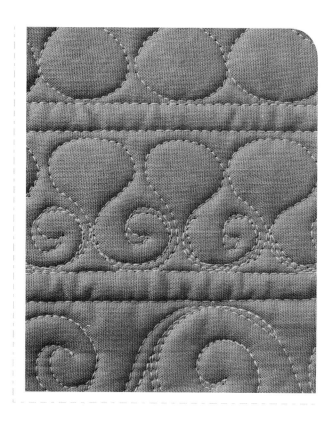

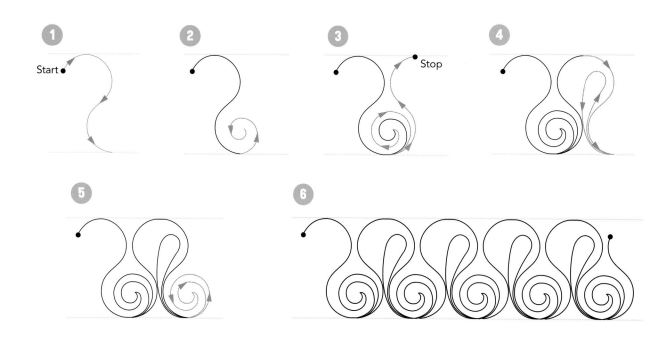

Archways

Archways are fun and easy to quilt, and they are a perfect motif in small borders, in sashing, or for filling a channel that you created with a longarm ruler. A channel is the area between two lines of straight stitching, and it can be curved or straight. Archways also work well with curved piecing designs such as medallions.

1 Start at the bottom of your border, as indicated, and quilt a circular bubble or bump that is similar in shape to an archway in a door (**FIGURE 1**).

2 Travel up the line you just finished and make another archway (**FIGURE 2**).

3 Maintain a consistent size and continue along the entire border or space you are filling with the archways (**FIGURE 3**).

GO CIRCULAR

Archways also look great when stitched around a circle. You can use these in circular designs or create your own medallion quilting in some negative space. I will demonstrate this technique in Chapter 3, Doodling and Drawing.

Feathers

Feathers are usually considered a traditional quilting motif, but they are so much fun to use in a modern way. You can add echoes, back-and-forth lines, or other modern shapes; or you can make big feather plumes. I will show you a basic feather shape that's easy to quilt. It will take some practice to get the shape and feel of quilting feathers, but I promise you it is totally worth the effort.

1 Start by quilting a long curvy line for the spine (**FIGURE 1**).

2 Echo the line back to where you started (**FIGURE 2**).

3 On the side of the spine you just quilted, quilt a feather petal by making a shape similar to the paisley design (**FIGURE 3**).

4 Travel back along the feather petal you just quilted and make another feather petal (**FIGURE 4**).

5 Continue making petals along the side of the spine until you reach the end (**FIGURE 5**).

6 Either travel back down the spine to the starting point or tie off, move your machine, and resume quilting at the starting point. Sometimes on a long border, tying off is easier, is faster, and looks neater (**FIGURE 6**).

7 Make feather petals on the other side of the spine (**FIGURE 7**).

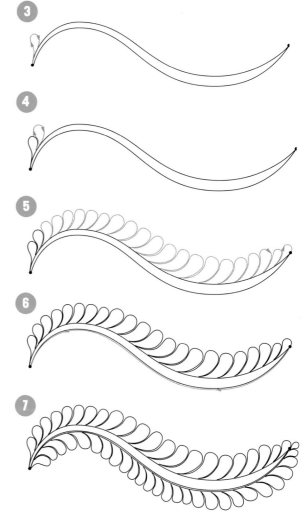

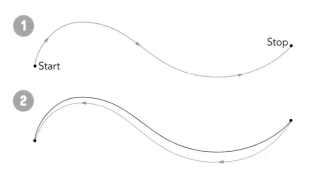

ECHO FEATHERS

Once you have a complete feather, you can echo the feather for an alternative look. The echoing gives you a closed design that works well to add back-and-forth lines or pebbles to really make your feather pop.

1 Quilt all your feather petals up one side and echo back down to the starting point (**FIGURE 1**).

2 Quilt your feather petals up the other side of the spine and echo back down (**FIGURE 2**).

3 Now, if desired, you can add some back-and-forth lines on either side of your feather (**FIGURE 3**).

4 Another option is to add some pebbles to really pop that feather (**FIGURE 4**).

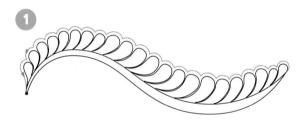

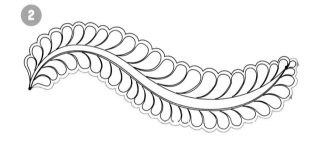

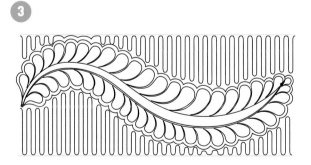

SWIRL FEATHERS

The swirl feather can be used to fill in large areas of open space. It can also work as an allover motif for an entire quilt. It's very easy to move from one feather swirl to another space simply by echoing until you get to the new area.

1 Start by quilting a swirl and returning to where you started (**FIGURE 1**).

2 Add feather petals around the side of the swirl (**FIGURE 2**).

3 Echo around the petals back down to the start of your swirl (**FIGURE 3**).

4 Make another swirl shape where you just finished (**FIGURE 4**).

5 Add feather petals and echo back to the start (**FIGURE 5**).

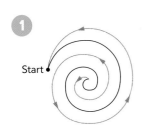

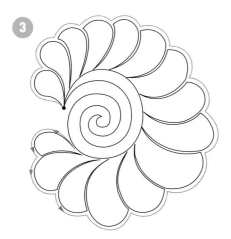

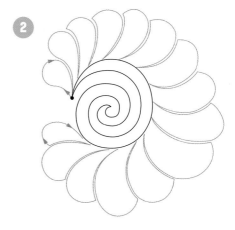

6 Continue making swirls with feather petals. If you get stuck and need to travel to another area, echo the feather petals once more or follow another swirl out (**FIGURE 6**).

7 Feather swirl the entire area where you are working, traveling around with echoing as needed. Your feather swirls will be going in all directions (**FIGURE 7**).

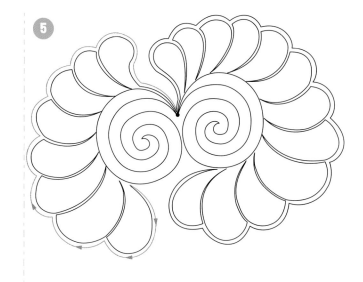

Straight Line

Simple straight-line quilting is a nice way to set off other motifs such as feathers and swirls. Use a straightedge longarm ruler and the lines on the ruler to keep the stitched lines the same distance apart. Again, it takes practice with a longarm ruler to achieve accurate straight lines.

Straight lines work great if you have a quilt where the fabrics or the pieced design is the star. The straight lines keep the quilting on the blocks simple while still holding the quilt sandwich together nicely. Blocks such as flying geese, square boxes, star blocks, and borders go particularly well with straight lines.

1 Start in the bottom left-hand corner. Using a straightedge ruler, quilt a straight line from the bottom left to the top right corner. Travel down the block or seam to the bottom right corner. Quilt a straight line to the top left of the block (**FIGURE 1**).

2 From here, quilt to the middle of the square, stopping ¼" to ½" (6 mm to 1.3 cm) from the center. Quilt to the opposite side of block and then echo back in the opposite direction. Complete the block by traveling down the side of the block until you complete all four sides (**FIGURE 2**).

MAKING STRAIGHT LINES WITH CHANNEL LOCKS

For straight-line quilting on an entire quilt, load the quilt and set the channel locks on your longarm. Channel locks prevent the machine from moving vertically or horizontally depending on how you set it up. I load my quilt the direction I want the horizontal lines to go; this might mean loading my quilt sideways. Once the channel lock is set, you can stitch a perfectly straight line without a ruler. You can space the lines out by making tick marks every ½" to ¾" (1.3 to 2 cm) on the side of your quilt. Continue to stitch the lines across the entire quilt. This is actually a pretty fast process and makes for a modern, clean design.

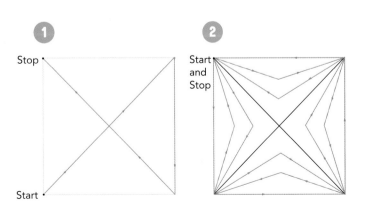

Beadboard

Beadboard quilting is awesome in a wide border or on a masculine quilt. You make it using your straightedge longarm ruler.

1 Quilt a straight line going down to the bottom of your space (**FIGURE 1**).

2 Move your ruler over ¼" (6 mm) and quilt another line going up to the top of the space (**FIGURE 2**).

3 Decide how wide you want the spacing on your beadboard. I usually go with 1½" (3.8 cm). Travel the desired width across the top of your space and quilt a line down (**FIGURE 3**).

4 Move your ruler over ¼" (6 mm) and quilt another line up to the top of the border (**FIGURE 4**).

5 Continue alternating the two widths across the entire space (**FIGURE 5**).

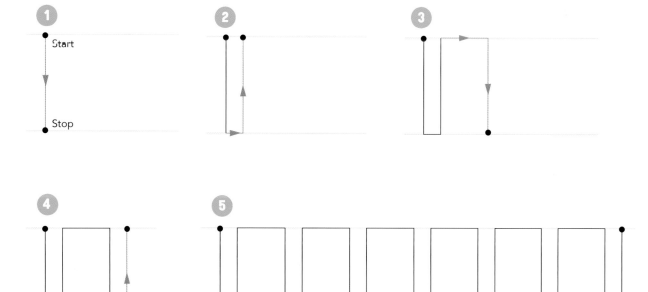

Back-and-Forth Lines

Back-and-forth lines are a great way to do some dense quilting around a motif or a design that you really want to stand out, such as a feather, a row of pebbles, or a center medallion. The key is to make sure your design is closed—you don't want any breaks or openings in the stitching that creates the design. You have to quilt the back-and-forth lines right next to the stitches of the design, and if there are gaps, the back-and-forth lines actually blend into the design, and it won't pop.

If you aren't sure if a design is closed, take the time to echo around the outside of your design or motif and then add the back-and-forth lines. Feathers, which look closed, have small spaces between the individual petals and will appear lost in the back-and-forth quilting. The small amount of space between the echo and the feather helps the feather really stand out.

1 Start on the left side of the space. Use a straight longarm ruler to quilt a line straight down. Then curve to the right just a little (**FIGURE 1**).

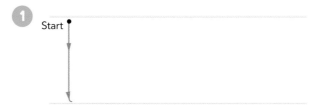

2 Stitch a straight line upward and curve slightly to the right at the top of the space. Continue stitching lines up and down. Keep the lines as close and as consistently spaced as you can. Use the straight longarm ruler as needed to keep the lines straight (**FIGURE 2**).

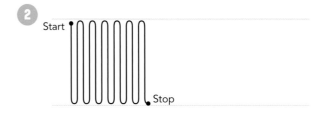

Squares

The square motif works well for quilting in large areas without having to stop and start. Use them in square or rectangular sections formed by the piecing in patchwork quilts, blocks, or borders. For a border, measure the length and figure how many inches each square needs to be to make them all the same size. I like my squares to be 4" to 5" (10 to 12.5 cm). Mark evenly spaced lines based on your measurements and use those lines for reference as you are quilting the squares. If you have square blocks, use those as your registration lines.

1 Quilt a large square clockwise, following the arrows. You will stop short of the starting point. The distance between where you stop and the starting point will be your spacing for the rest of the spiraling square (**FIGURE 1**).

2 Continue quilting successive squares clockwise until you get to the center of the square. Remember to keep your lines straight—feel free to use a longarm ruler to help you—and to maintain your spacing. You will end in the center of the square (**FIGURE 2**).

3 To continue to your next space, stitch a line to the right of the first square you just quilted. Quilt a line going down and continue to make another square (**FIGURE 3**).

4 Continue along your row in this same manner, alternating the direction of each square. (**FIGURE 4**).

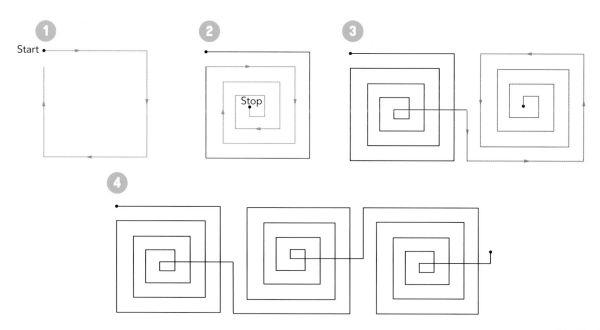

Greek Key

A Greek key creates a fun, clean, modern look that is great either in big blocks of large-print or novelty fabric or to fill in square pieced blocks. It is similar to the square motif except that it is designed for an individual block or space. It is not meant for continuous quilting, so you won't quilt a line to get out of the motif. When making this motif, it's beneficial to keep the spacing even. I usually try to keep my lines spaced ¼" to ½" (6 mm to 1.3 cm) apart.

1 Using a straightedge longarm ruler, start at one corner of the block about ¼" to ½" (6 mm to 1.3 cm) from the side. Quilt a line around the entire block as shown, going in a clockwise direction and stopping just short of the starting point (**FIGURE 1**).

2 Continue echoing the previous lines, using your hopping foot or a longarm ruler as a guide to keep the spacing even (**FIGURE 2**).

3 Keep echoing around the square until you get to the center of the block. End the quilting here and tie off the thread (**FIGURE 3**).

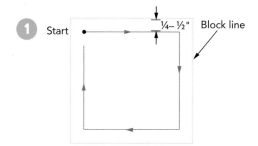

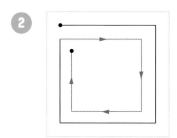

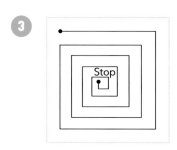

TYING OFF THREAD

There are a couple ways to tie off your thread when you have a place you need to stop on your quilt. You can simply take a couple very small stitches to secure the ends and then pull up your bobbin thread and cut the threads. This is my preferred method. You can also bury your threads if you are so inclined. To do this, thread the ends onto a hand-sewing needle, then push the needle into the quilt top at the point where the threads come out of the quilt. Push the needle only into the batting (not the backing) and back up through the top away from where you started. Finally, cut the thread ends close to the fabric.

Maze-Style Background

Maze-style background is a fun fill to do freehand or with a longarm quilt ruler. Once you figure out how these are made, you'll likely just want to freehand them. This motif is very forgiving, and you can move from place to place very easily just by traveling up a previous quilting line. The trick is to maintain even spacing between the quilted lines.

1 Quilt a square (**FIGURE 1**).

2 Travel back over the top of your square and stitch past the square about ¼" (6 mm). Quilt a line that echoes the side and bottom of the square (**FIGURE 2**).

3 Stitch down from the previous line about ¼" (6 mm), echo the bottom and side, and then stitch back to the top of the square until you touch a previous line or the edge of the area (**FIGURE 3**).

4 Now the fun begins. Continue to quilt around the square and stop in a different location this time. There really is no right or wrong with this design, and that's what I love about it (**FIGURE 4**).

5 Quilt around your top, creating maze shapes by traveling up and down previous lines. You can make the mazes look like they are coming out of each other (**FIGURE 5**).

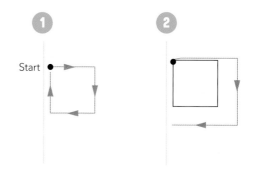

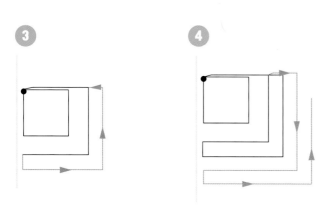

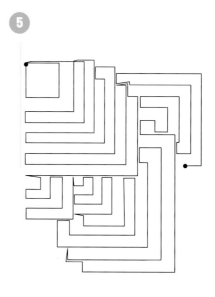

CHAPTER **3**

DOODLING
& DRAWING

DOODLING & DRAWING

Quilting is much easier once it becomes intuitive, and doodling can help with developing that ability. Doodling is not only a great way to learn new designs; it can help you improve your hand-eye coordination, which is essential to longarm quilting.

The more you think about what you're doing the harder it will be, so it's good to just relax and let the quilting happen. I quilt best when I get in my "quilting zone," where I'm in my own world, and the quilting feels natural and free. The process becomes fluid, and my brain knows where to go with the design

almost without me consciously thinking about it. This happens partly because I practice a lot on paper, and I mean a lot! I doodle all the time: while making dinner, watching television, talking on the telephone, and riding in the car. There is always time to doodle, even if only during the few free moments you have in a day. As a bonus, it's very relaxing to sit and draw out designs, and sometimes the doodles turn out pretty amazing. You will find that once you draw something and get the flow of the design, you can easily take it from paper to fabric.

Doodling on Paper

My favorite way to doodle is to start with a design I can make well, such as a basic swirl. Then I keep adding other designs, and pretty soon I have something amazing.

As you doodle on paper in preparation for longarm quilting, choose designs from Chapter 2 to incorporate into your drawing. While practicing, remember to keep your pen on the paper; you don't want to have starts and stops, just like with longarm quilting. This is excellent training for traveling, which is a longarm quilting term for following along previously quilted lines to easily make your way around the quilt with the longarm machine. In the end, all this practice will make quilting more enjoyable and a lot quicker while creating the necessary muscle memory needed for good hand-eye coordination.

From Paper to Fabric

When you're ready to try your hand at doodling with the longarm machine, I recommend practicing on a whole-cloth quilt. As the name implies, a whole-cloth quilt has a solid piece of fabric for the top rather than a pieced top. Typically, the quilting designs are quilted with tone-on-tone threads. These are usually traditional-style quilts and involve very exquisite designs and lots of feathers, pebbles, and dense quilting.

For your practice purposes, however, a whole-cloth quilt serves as a beautiful way to show off what you've learned. Quilt your designs, and when you're finished, you will have a whole cloth that you can bind and use as a table runner or wall quilt. The bonus is it will be fun to look at a year down the road and see how far you have come.

Remember that these are for practice, and you're going to learn from your mistakes. I promise you if you practice enough, you will get better. Don't be hard on yourself. We quilt for fun!

HANG YOUR QUILTS

I like hanging my quilts on the walls of my home. The pieces really are works of art, so why not put them on display? Try hanging your quilts with hand-sewing needles—just use a small hammer to tap the needle into the wall. The fine needles won't leave much of a mark on the wall, yet they are sturdy enough to hold a small quilt.

FINISHED SIZE: 30" × 40" (76 × 101.5 cm)

Doodles
TABLE TOPPER

In this practice project, you'll doodle with the longarm machine just as you doodled on paper. You won't need any registration marks. Just start in the left corner of the fabric and quilt your way through the entire piece in free-form fashion. For this example, I used a thread color that blends with the fabric for a pretty tone-on-tone look.

1 Cut a piece of solid fabric 30" × 40" (76 × 101.5 cm) for the quilt top. Do not mark the top. Load the quilt sandwich onto the machine. Start in the top left corner of the quilt sandwich and quilt a simple design that you're comfortable making. For this table topper, I first quilted a simple swirl motif (page 33).

2 Quilt different designs as you continue into the quilt sandwich. I practiced a big flower in the center of my quilt sandwich and added pebbles (page 36), echoed ribbon candy (page 41), clamshells (page 39), paisleys (page 38), feathers (page 44), and maze-style background (page 53). Feel free to throw them all in. Just have fun playing. You can't go wrong, and I promise you, it's a gorgeous quilt to have once you're finished.

3 Remove the quilt from the frame, trim the edges, and add binding. Now you have a usable whole-cloth table topper.

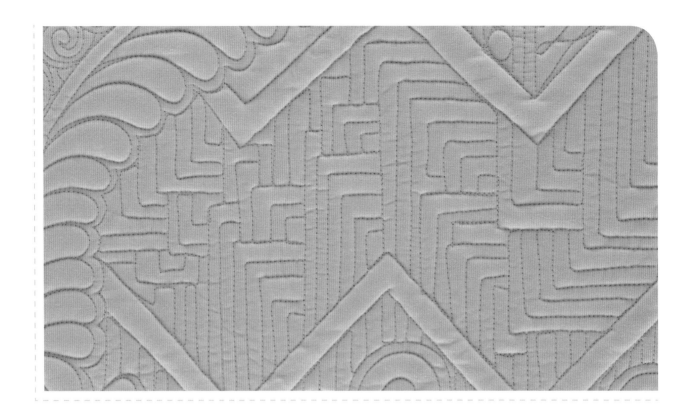

Doodling
in Shapes

Another approach to doodle quilting is to draw
shapes that you then fill with doodles. It's lots of fun
to grab some rulers and your favorite marking pens
to draw a basic plan before you load your fabric on
the longarm. Just draw your design elements, such
as circles, squares, triangles, diamonds, hexagons,
or maybe some grids onto the top. I like to use a
Mark-B-Gone blue water-soluble pen to mark the
designs. You can use your curved rulers to make
scallop shapes, or use your straight rulers to create
grids, stars, and channels. You can also use things
around your house to create shape templates.
Place paper plates, pots, or pans onto cardboard or
cardstock and trace around the items. Cut out the
shapes with scissors and use these templates again
and again.

1   Cut a piece of solid fabric to your desired size for the quilt top. To start, divide your quilt top into fourths, either by pressing lines into your fabric with an iron or using marking tools to draw registration lines (**FIGURE 1**). These lines will help you keep the motifs evenly spaced as you create your design.

2   Now use a longarm circle ruler with your fabric-marking tool to draw a perfect circle in the center of your fabric (**FIGURE 2**).

3   Build on this design by drawing more circles on your fabric (**FIGURE 3**).

4   Use your rulers to add some straight lines to your circles to create stars. The possibilities are endless (**FIGURE 4**).

5   When you've drawn all of your shapes, quilt some of the filler designs you learned in Chapter 2 inside these empty shapes (**FIGURE 5**).

6   Remove the quilt from the frame, trim the edges, and add binding.

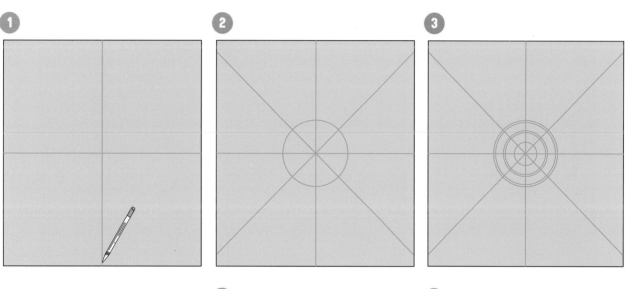

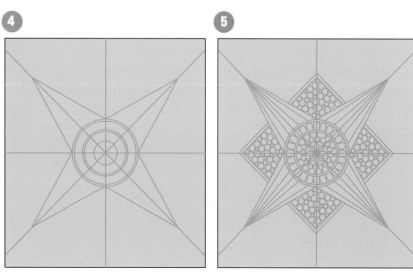

ECHOING

I like to echo the shapes with a ¼" (6 mm) line around each design to set them apart from the background quilting.

On-Point
SQUARE
TABLE RUNNER

For this piece, I did a little preplanning and marking to make an on-point square filled with smaller designs. Again, I used a matching thread, which helped to hide the mistakes and gave the table runner an attractive tone-on-tone appearance.

1 Cut a piece of solid fabric 20" × 30" (51 × 76 cm) for the quilt top. Find the center of the fabric and mark registration lines. Draw a square on the diagonal in the center of the fabric with a water-soluble marking pen, using the registration lines as guides (**FIGURE 1**). There's no need to mark all the quilting; just mark the square outlines.

2 When you are happy with the bones of the design, load the quilt sandwich.

3 Start in the center of this piece because it's a small table runner. I would not start in the center of a larger piece because it can create wrinkles and puckers. Quilt the straight lines of the squares and then go back and fill in the spaces with dense quilting designs. For this example, I used archways (page 43), straight lines (page 48), ribbon candy (page 40), double bubbles (page 37), and swirls (page 33). Note: Registration lines are only drawn and not actually stitched.

4 Remove the quilt from the frame, trim the edges, and add binding.

Figure 1

FINISHED SIZE: 24" × 42" (61 × 106.5 cm)

Scalloped
CENTER
TABLE RUNNER

This example illustrates how to create a secondary design—in this case zigzags—behind your main design, to add dimension. This project is also great for practicing filler designs, which give the background its interest.

1 Cut a piece of solid fabric 24" × 42" (61 × 106.5 cm) for the quilt top. For registration lines, use a water-soluble marking pen and a straightedge ruler to draw a grid with 3" (7.5 cm) squares. Use curved rulers to create the large arcs for the curved shape in the center (**FIGURE 1**).

2 Draw the on-point square in the center of the quilt, using the grid as a guide (**FIGURE 2**).

3 Draw the zigzag lines behind the center shape, again using the grid as a guide (**FIGURE 3**).

Figure 1

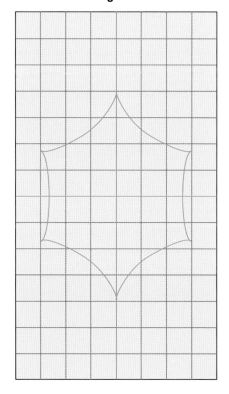

4 Load the quilt sandwich. Start by quilting the center square, the curved shape, and the lines of the zigzags running in the background. Go back and fill in these areas with a variety of quilting designs. I used pebbles (page 36), swirls (page 33), straight lines (page 48), maze-style background (page 53), ribbon candy (page 40), feathers (page 44), and back-and-forth lines (page 50). As you can see, I quilted every little inch of this top.

5 Remove the quilt from the frame, trim the edges, and add binding.

Figure 2

Figure 3

FINISHED SIZE: 40" × 40" (101.5 × 101.5 cm)

Modern Medallion
STAR
WALL QUILT

Let's try a more complex sample now. This whole cloth looks intimidating, but it really isn't once you see how it is laid out. Just take it step by step. Cream or white fabric makes such a beautiful statement for a whole cloth. Either color really shows the texture of the quilting and makes for an elegant wall quilt.

1 Cut a piece of solid fabric 40" × 40" (101.5 × 101.5 cm) for the quilt top. Find the center of the fabric by folding the fabric in half and pressing the fold with an iron. Fold the fabric again, in fourths, and press the fold. Open the fabric and mark the fold lines with a water-soluble marker.

2 Using a water-soluble marker, draw 2 diagonal lines through the center.

3 Use circle rulers to mark the largest circle around the center. Align the registration marks on the ruler with the ones on the quilt to perfectly center the circle. Mark successively smaller circles within the large circle to create channels (**FIGURE 1**). I use a series of circle

Figure 1

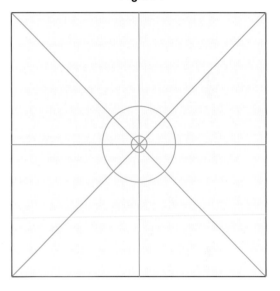

rulers that decrease in size by ½" to 1" (1.3 to 2.5 cm) increments. I used an 11½" (29 cm) ruler for the largest circle and a 2½" (6.5 cm) ruler for the smallest circle.

4 Find the center between each adjacent pair of registration lines and mark the point on the outermost circle.

5 From the outer edge of the circle, measure 7" (18 cm) up each registration line and make a mark. With straight lines, connect the marks all the way around the circle to make 8 star points (**FIGURE 2**).

6 Load the quilt onto the longarm. Stitch the medallion in the center of the star. Add the filler designs of archways (page 43), pebbles (page 36), and ribbon candy (page 40) in each channel.

7 Stitch the points of the star. Stitch equally spaced peaks inside each star point, using the registration lines as a guide. I added 5 peaks to each star point. Echo the star with a ¼" (6 mm) line.

8 Get creative and add some curves between the star points, using the registration lines as guides. Echo the curves with a ¼" (6 mm) line. Instead of this secondary design behind the star, you could try straight lines or maybe a square.

9 Create a design of curves and points around the star and echo with a ¼" (6 mm) line. Add feathers (page 44) to the outer edge.

10 Finally, fill the remaining areas with dense filler motifs, including double-line diagonal grids, swirls (page 33), and pebbles.

11 Remove the quilt from the frame, trim the edges, and bind.

Figure 2

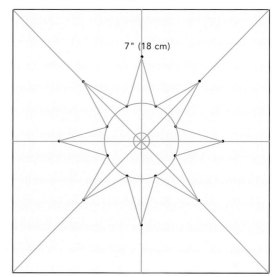

7" (18 cm)

CIRCLE RULERS

When purchasing circle rulers, make sure to get ones with registration lines printed on them. Usually rulers have registration marks. The registration lines are critical for perfectly placed circles.

Medallion
STARS
LAP QUILT

This is my favorite whole cloth that I've ever designed. I used an aqua solid fabric with matching aqua thread. The key to quilting a whole-cloth design is to repeat design elements. The repeated designs in this piece are the stars, which I drew on the fabric before quilting. Other than the stars, the designs are pretty random and free-form.

1 Cut a piece of solid fabric 45" × 70" (114.5 × 178 cm) for the quilt top. Mark registration lines on the quilt for the large and small stars. Begin by drawing circles with your circle rulers and then add smaller circles inside the larger circles for the medallions (**FIGURE 1**). Use the registration lines to align your circles evenly and to figure out the spacing on your whole cloth.

Figure 1

2 Make the stars by using a straight ruler and adding outer points to the circles. Follow the instructions in Steps 3–5 for the Modern Medallion Star Wall Quilt, pages 71–72. Mark an outline for those straight lines with a ¼" (6 mm) line. Vary the number of points to the stars. Here, I have 8 points on some stars and 4 points on others (**FIGURE 2**).

3 Draw random zigzag lines to break up the areas for quilting (**FIGURE 3**). This separation makes a great transition area for you to change out designs.

4 After the bones of your design are complete, load the quilt sandwich and begin working in sections of the quilt. I quilted small sections of stars first and then went back and added the dense filler designs around the stars and straight-line (page 48) zigzag areas.

5 Remove the quilt from the frame, trim the edges, and add binding.

Figure 2

Figure 3

CHAPTER 4
PIECED
PROJECTS

PIECED
PROJECTS

In the previous chapter, you learned how to quilt whole-cloth motifs. Most of these designs were drawn on the fabric in a layout of your choosing. In this chapter, you'll learn to quilt motifs on pieced projects.

Here are three easy-to-sew projects that will go together quickly, so that you can practice some of your new longarm quilting skills. The projects feature a variety of pieces shapes—rectangles, triangles, hexagons—for you to quilt, plus plenty of open spaces for you to try some larger motifs or create secondary designs.

I encourage you to make the projects and not worry about the quality of the quilting. The more you practice, the better you will get, so enjoy the process and have fun!

What to Quilt Where

The process for quilting a pieced quilt is different from quilting a whole cloth because you need to take cues from the pieced top. First, look at the quilt and determine the style of the quilt top: traditional or modern. For traditional quilts, you might go with feathers, pebbles, straight lines, and stippling. For modern quilts, you might use more swirls, pebbles, and geometric motifs. There really are no rules. You can quilt traditional quilts with modern quilting or modern quilts with traditional quilting used in modern ways. It just depends on the quilt and your taste in quilting.

I am often asked why I quilted something the way I did. Honestly, I have to say I just quilt what looks good to me. When I first started quilting, I struggled with this process. It helped me to take a photo of the quilt, print out the photo, and practice drawing motifs right on the quilt image.

It's also helpful to look closely at the block design. If you have a quilt that has twenty-four of the same block, all you really have to do is figure out how to quilt one block, and then repeat it twenty-three more times. Easy! It can seem overwhelming when you see a quilt in its entirety, but if you think about it as one block or one border, it's easy to figure out.

Then look to see if there are any secondary designs you can create with the blocks. Sometimes all it takes is looking at the seam lines of the piecing. You can often come up with fun secondary designs by just following the block seams and echoing them. The seams make excellent reference lines, and you don't have to do any marking. You will find squares, hexagons, diamonds, and endless other shapes you can reference.

Next, separate the quilt into sections and decide how you will quilt each section. The sections might be borders, individual blocks, groups of blocks, or areas you created with the secondary designs. Sectioning the quilt helps me from being overwhelmed with the entire quilt. If you break the quilt down into sections and do the same consistent quilting throughout the quilt, it's not such a daunting task.

Once you determined your quilt sections, it's time to load the quilt and get quilting. Use what you've learned in previous chapters to fill in the lines with dense filler or geometric motifs, and mix in some straight-line ruler work to create more secondary designs. The best approach is to try not to overthink the quilting and just go with your gut instincts. If you prefer, you can mark the motifs on your quilt. You can always spray away the marks if you don't like a certain motif or the overall design.

In the Ventana quilt (page 114), the white areas make a secondary design behind the block shapes. I stitched in the ditch around the blocks and then quilted an echo in the background shape and filled it with swirls. I love how it shows off the shape of the secondary design.

FINISHED SIZE: 55" × 61" (139.5 × 155 cm)

Snicker Doodle
QUILT

I made this project using the Hex N More and the Sidekick rulers by Julie Herman of Jaybird Quilts. You can make the quilt with a traditional ruler with 30- and 60-degree markings; however, Julie's rulers make quick work of the cutting.

I made two versions of this quilt and quilted them differently to show you there really is no wrong way to quilt a quilt. I encourage you to try different ways to quilt your practice pieces. I can't wait to see your version of this quilt.

MATERIALS

5 fat quarters (18" × 20" [45.5 × 51 cm] each) for star points

2½" × 3" (6.5 × 7.5 cm) scraps for center hexagons or use leftover pieces from fat quarters

2½ yards (2.3 m) white fabric for background and middle border

⅓ yard (30.5 cm) green fabric for inner border

¾ yard (0.7 m) aqua fabric for outer border

3½ yards (3.2 m) fabric for backing

½ yard (0.5 m) fabric for binding

61" × 67" (155 × 170 cm) piece of batting

Jaybird Quilts Mini Hex N More or Hex N More ruler

Jaybird Quilts Sidekick or Super Sidekick ruler

Cutting

FAT QUARTERS

From each fat quarter, cut one strip 3½" × 21"
(9 × 53.5 cm).

Sub-cut 6 notched star-point triangles with the
Sidekick ruler.

1 At the right end of a 3½" (9 cm) strip, align the
Sidekick ruler to the bottom edge. The solid
horizontal 3½" line will align with the top of the
strip. Cut along the right edge of the ruler to
trim the strip (**FIGURE 1**).

2 Rotate the fabric strip 180 degrees.

3 Flip the ruler over to the back side. Align the
ruler to the top edge of the strip and align the
cut edge of the fabric strip with the 3½" (9 cm)
line. Cut along the right edge of the ruler to
complete the triangle (**FIGURE 2**).

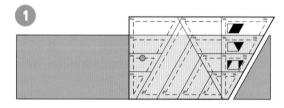

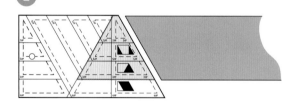

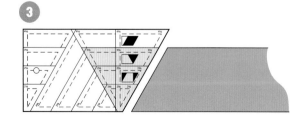

4 Flip the ruler to the front side and cut the next triangle (**FIGURE 3**).

5 Repeat the previous steps to cut 6 notched star-point triangles from the strip.

SCRAPS

From your 2½" × 3" (6.5 × 7.5 cm) scraps, cut 30 hexagon shapes.

1 Align the top of either the Mini Hex N More ruler or the Hex N More ruler with the top of a rectangle (**FIGURE 4**).

2 Cut along both edges of the ruler to trim the rectangle and cut a hexagon (**FIGURE 5**).

WHITE BACKGROUND FABRIC

Cut 6 strips 5" × WOF (width of fabric) (12.5 cm × WOF). Set aside for middle borders.

Cut 3 strips 1½" × WOF (3.8 cm × WOF).

Sub-cut 90 triangles with your (Mini) Hex N More or (Super) Sidekick ruler. All four rulers will work for this step. You should get 33 triangles per strip.

1 Using the Mini Hex N More ruler or the Hex N More ruler, align either ruler along the top and bottom edges of the strip. Cut along both edges of the ruler to trim the strip and cut the first triangle (**FIGURE 6**).

2 Rotate the ruler 180 degrees to cut the next triangle (**FIGURE 7**).

3 Repeat Steps 1 and 2 to continue cutting the triangles. Each strip will yield 33 triangles. Repeat steps to cut a total of 90 triangles.

Cut 6 strips 3½" × WOF (9 cm × WOF).

Sub-cut 80 triangles with your Sidekick ruler. You should get 15 per strip. Use the instructions for cutting the fat quarter triangles above to cut these strips.

Cut 2 strips 3½" × WOF (9 cm × WOF).

Cut 20 right half triangles with your Sidekick Ruler.

Cut 20 left half triangles with your Sidekick ruler.

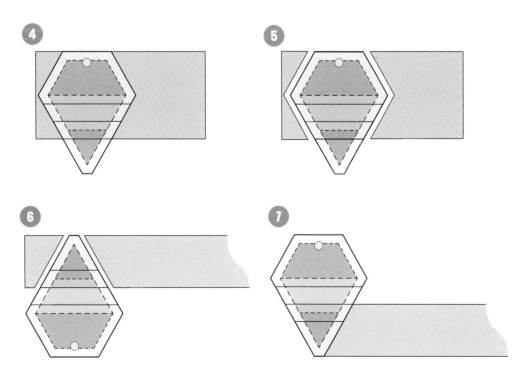

1 To cut both right and left half triangles at once, keep the fabric folded with the selvedges together. Use a ruler to remove the selvedges and create a clean square edge (**FIGURE 8**).

2 Align the edge of the ruler to the bottom edge of the strip, the vertical solid line to the left edge of the strip, and the solid horizontal 3½" (9 cm) line to the top edge of the fabric strip. Cut along the right edge of the ruler to cut a left and a right half triangle (**FIGURE 9**).

3 Rotate the ruler 180 degrees and align the cut edges with the 3½" (9 cm) lines. Cut along the right edge of the ruler to cut the next 2 half triangles (**FIGURE 10**).

4 Repeat the previous steps to cut a total of 20 right and 20 left half triangles (**FIGURE 11**).

Cut 2 strips 12½" × WOF (31.5 cm × WOF).

Sub-cut 4 pieces 12½" × 14½" (31.5 cm × 37 cm) for your blocks. You will get 2 per strip. Note: Measure your pieced blocks and cut your pieces according to the size of those blocks.

GREEN FABRIC

Cut 5 strips 2" × WOF (5 cm × WOF) of green fabric. Set aside for inner borders.

AQUA FABRIC

Cut 6 strips 4" × WOF (10 cm × WOF) of aqua fabric. Set aside for outer borders.

BINDING

Cut 7 strips 2¼" × WOF (5.5 cm × WOF) of binding fabric. Set aside.

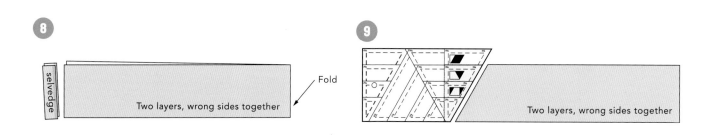

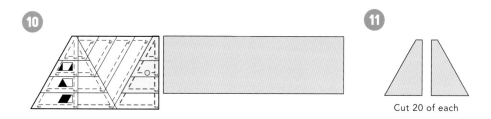

Cut 20 of each

Assembly

Use a ¼" (6 mm) seam allowance.

SEW TRIANGLES AND HEXAGONS

1 Begin by sewing triangles to 3 sides of a hexagon. Arrange a hexagon and three 1½" (3.8 cm) triangles as shown (**FIGURE 12**).

2 Place the triangles on the hexagon, right sides together. Align the notched corner of the triangle with every other edge of the hexagon (**FIGURE 13**).

3 Sew seams and press open (**FIGURE 14**). Make 30.

SEW HALF LEFT AND RIGHT TRIANGLES

1 Arrange a left half triangle and a right half triangle as shown. Sew the half triangles together and press the seams open (**FIGURE 15**). Make 20.

2 Arrange a 3½" (9 cm) triangle as shown to create a larger *left* half triangle. Sew the seam, and then press the seam open (**FIGURE 16**). Make 10.

3 Arrange a 3½" (9 cm) triangle as shown to create a larger *right* half triangle. Sew the seam and then press the seam open (**FIGURE 17**). Make 10.

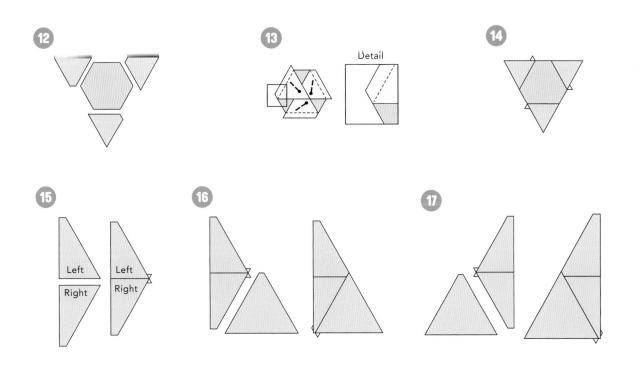

ASSEMBLE BLOCKS

1 On a design wall or large surface, arrange the sewn blocks and the notched 3½" (9 cm) triangles as shown in the diagram (**FIGURE 18**).

2 Sew a star-point triangle to a pieced center block and press the seam open. Add a background triangle to each side of the star-point triangle and press the seam open (**FIGURE 10**). Make 6 for each block, 30 total.

3 Your block should look like this (**FIGURE 20**).

4 Sew 3 large triangle units together and press the seams open. Add a left side piece and a right side piece to complete the row and press the seams open (**FIGURE 21**).

5 Repeat as shown for the second row (**FIGURE 22**).

6 Sew the 2 rows together. Take extra care to align all seams. Press seams open. You now have a block that is about 14½" × 12½" (37 × 31.5 cm). Make a total of 5 blocks.

7 Measure your blocks and cut the background pieces the same size.

ASSEMBLE QUILT TOP

1 Lay out your quilt blocks as shown to create a large Nine Patch (**FIGURE 23**). Note that the pieced blocks are rotated 90 degrees from the orientation they were shown as they were pieced.

2 Sew blocks to create 3 rows. Press the seams away from the pieced block.

3 Sew 3 rows together and press the seams open to complete the middle of the quilt top.

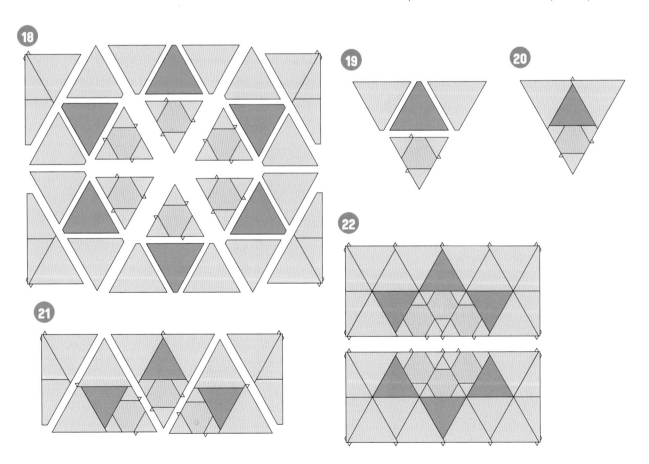

ADD BORDERS

1 Cut one of the green 2" × WOF (5 cm × WOF) border strips in half. Join the half strip to a full border strip diagonally at the ends to make 2 side borders.

2 Measure the quilt top vertically through the center. Trim the 2 green side borders to that length. Sew the green borders to the sides of the quilt top.

3 Measure the quilt top horizontally through the center. Trim the green top and bottom borders to that length. Sew the green borders to the top and bottom of the quilt top.

4 Cut one of the white 5" × WOF (12.5 cm × WOF) border strips in half. Join the half strip to a full border strip diagonally at the ends to make 2 side borders.

5 Repeat Steps 2 and 3 to sew on the white middle border strips.

6 Cut one of the aqua 4" × WOF (10 cm × WOF) border strips in half. Join the half strip to a full border strip diagonally at the ends to make 2 side borders.

7 Repeat Steps 2 and 3 to sew on the aqua outer border strips (**FIGURE 24**).

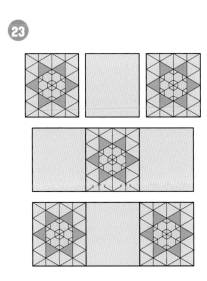

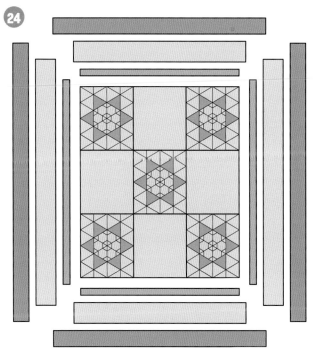

Quilt Assembly

BORDER TIP

When adding borders, it is essential that your top is square so you don't have wavy borders. Measure your quilt through the center both vertically and horizontally and then use these measurements for the top, bottom, and side borders. Align and pin the ends and centers before sewing to avoid uneven borders.

Quilting and Finishing

Now you are ready to load this beauty up and have some quilting fun!

1 If you'd like to quilt this version of the Snicker Doodle Quilt in the same way I did, follow these instructions. Note: I marked the diamonds in the background blocks on the machine. If you prefer, you can mark the diamonds before the quilt is loaded by following the instructions in Steps 6 and 7 below.

2 Load the quilt with the width horizontal to the rollers. Start in the top left corner and work from left to right. Quilt as much as you can in the available areas of the quilt and then roll or advance the quilt top.

3 In the outer border, quilt square designs (page 51) 3¾" (9.5 cm) apart. This is the width of the border, so it ensures the squares will be square. You may need to slightly adjust the spacing between the squares to fill the length of the border evenly. You can freehand quilt these squares or use a ruler. I usually just freehand them because it's faster, but it takes time to learn how to quilt straight lines without a ruler. Complete as many squares as you can down the side border with the quilt positioned as it is. When you advance the quilt to work in different areas, continue to quilt the side borders.

4 With the quilt still in its first position, quilt echo feathers (page 45) in the white border and curve the feathers into the corner and down as much of the right border as you can quilt in the available throat space. Quilt some back-and-forth lines (page 50) on both sides of the feathers to really make your feathers pop.

Each time you advance the quilt, continue this feather border, making it appear to go around the quilt in one direction from left to right.

5 In the inner green border, quilt a simple ribbon candy motif (page 40) along the top only. When the rest of the quilt is quilted, you will go back and finish the sides and bottom of this border in one fluid motion without stops and starts.

28

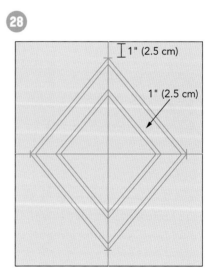

1" (2.5 cm)

1" (2.5 cm)

6 By this time, you should have advanced your quilt enough to be toward the center area, which has the blocks. With the quilt still loaded on the machine, draw diagonal lines from corner to corner in each of the background blocks with your marking tools. Then draw a horizontal and a vertical line through the center to determine the center of the block.

7 Measure down 1" (2.5 cm) from each straight line. Using a straightedge longarm ruler, quilt a line from each point you just marked and echo the line ¼" (6 mm) away. Create another diamond ¾" to 1" (2 cm to 2.5 cm) inside the first diamond and echo that line ¼" away (**FIGURE 28**). Fill in the center of the diamond with double bubbles (page 37), and quilt archways (page 43) in the larger ¾" space.

8 In the pieced star blocks, echo each star with a ¼" (6 mm) line. Stitch in the ditch around each star. This gives the stars definition and makes the blocks stand out from the background quilting.

9 Quilt triangle shapes in the outer points of the pieced stars and follow the shape for the inside of the star. Quilt a continuous line (page 26) around the center hexagon blocks.

10 Add swirls (page 33) in the negative space around the pieced blocks and the diamond secondary design.

11 Continue to quilt blocks and borders as you advance the quilt until you get to the end of the quilt.

12 Go back and finish the green border with the ribbon candy motif. Roll your quilt back to the beginning and quilt down the left border, across the bottom, up the right border, and end at the top right border.

13 Remove the quilt from the frame and trim the edges. Join the binding strips at the ends diagonally and bind the quilt using your favorite method.

FINISHED SIZE: 55" × 61" (139.5 × 155 cm)

Snicker Doodle
QUILT VARIATION

FABRICS: Chipper by Tula Pink

Here's another possible way you could quilt your Snicker Doodle Quilt. I wanted this quilt to look completely different than the first solid version of the quilt, so I chose a geometric motif for the background. Again, I didn't pre-mark anything for this quilt, but feel free to do so.

To quilt the quilt as I did, follow these steps.

1 Start in the top left-hand corner of your quilt. In the outer border, quilt a vertical line and echo that line ¼" (6 mm) away. Using your straightedge longarm ruler, space over ¾" (2 cm) and continue quilting a beadboard motif (page 49) based on this spacing. Quilt the top border and continue down the sides as you advance the quilt.

2 For the thick middle border, quilt echo ribbon candy (page 41). I quilted the top border only and then quilted the sides and bottom when the other quilting was complete.

3 In the inner border, quilt some wishbones (page 32).

4 For the pieced stars, echo the outside of each star block with a ¼" (6 mm) line and also stitch in the ditch (page 24) around each star. In the center of each hexagon, stitch overlapping petals to create a flower motif.

5 Create peaks in the outer star blocks with your straight ruler. Fill the negative spaces of the star blocks with wishbones.

6 In the open blocks, quilt a maze-style background motif (page 53) freehand—no rulers. This is a great way to practice quilting straight lines without a ruler. It doesn't have to be perfect. If you look closely, you will see my lines are not all straight. That just gives the quilt an organic look.

FINISHED SIZE: 50½" × 60½" (128.5 × 153.5 cm)

Delish
QUILT

This quilt got its name because it has so much room for delicious quilting. You've probably heard the phrase "Quilting makes the quilt" before, and in this case, it really does. This pattern is very simple and boring before the quilting. With quilting, you can add texture and design statements that take this little quilt to a new level. I used all solids to show how the quilting can really accent and add to the quilt top. Again, don't worry about your quilting being perfect. That is what is so great about this quilt top—it doesn't take a long time to piece, so that takes the worry out of possibly ruining a good quilt top. Just practice!

MATERIALS

⅝ yard (0.6 m) white fabric for center

½ yard (0.5 m) gray fabric for first border

¾ yard (0.7 m) aqua fabric for second border

1⅜ yards (1.3 m) turquoise fabric for third border

3¼ yards (3 m) fabric for backing

½ yard (0.5 m) fabric for binding

56" × 66" (142 × 167.5 cm) piece of batting

Cutting

CENTER

Cut a square 20" × 30" (51 × 76 cm) of white fabric.

INNER BORDER

Cut 4 strips 3½" × WOF (width of fabric) (9 cm × WOF) of gray fabric.

Sub-cut 2 strips 3½" × 30" (9 × 76 cm).

Sub-cut 2 strips 3½" × 26½" (9 × 67.5 cm).

MIDDLE BORDER

Cut 4 strips 5½" × WOF (14 cm × WOF) of aqua fabric.

Sub-cut 4 strips 5½" × 36½" (14 × 92.5 cm).

OUTER BORDER

Cut 6 strips 7½" × WOF (19 cm × WOF) of turquoise fabric.

Piece together strips to get 2 strips 7½" × 46½" (19 × 118 cm) and 2 strips 7½" × 50½" (19 × 128.5 cm).

BINDING

Cut 6 strips 2¼" × WOF (5.5 cm × WOF) of binding fabric. Set aside.

Assembly

Use a ¼" (6 mm) seam allowance.

1 Sew the 3½" × 30" (9 × 76 cm) gray inner border strips to the sides of the white center square. Press strips away from the center.

2 Sew the 3½" × 26½" (9 × 67.5 cm) gray inner border strips to the top and bottom of the white center. Press away from the center.

3 Measure the quilt top vertically through the center. Trim the length of the 5½" × 36½" (14 × 92.5 cm) aqua middle border strips to match. Sew to the sides of the quilt. Press away from the center.

4 Measure the quilt top horizontally through the center. Trim the length of the 5½" × 36½" (14 × 92.5 cm) aqua middle border strips to match. Sew to the top and bottom of the quilt. Press away from the center.

5 Measure the quilt top vertically through the center. Trim the length of the 7½" × 46½" (19 × 118 cm) turquoise outer border strips to match. Sew to the sides of the quilt. Press away from the center.

6 Measure the quilt top horizontally through the center. Trim the length of the 7½" × 50½" (19 × 128.5 cm) turquoise outer border strips to match. Sew to the top and bottom of the quilt. Press away from the center (**FIGURE 1**).

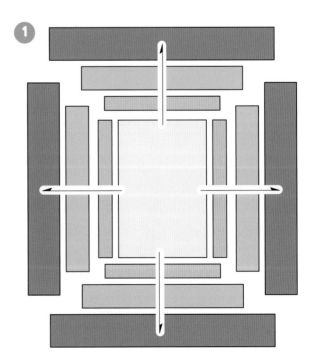

Quilting and Finishing

Your quilt is now ready for the fun part. Quilting! If you'd like to quilt it in the same way that I did, follow these steps.

1 Before loading the quilt, mark registration lines on the inner rectangle. Use a fabric marker to draw diagonal lines from corner to corner, then draw lines through the vertical and horizontal center. Use the registration lines as guides as you mark the concentric circles for the medallion. Draw a 2½" (6.5 cm) circle in the center followed by circles that are 3½" (9 cm), 5½" (14 cm), and 6½" (16.5 cm).

Draw scallops around the medallion, using a curved ruler; I used a size 15 QP Curve template by Linda Hrcka of The Quilted Pineapple. Draw an echo line ¼" (6 mm) away. Measure out 1" (2.5 cm) and mark another echo line and then mark one more line ¼" away (**FIGURE 2**).

2

2 Load the quilt with the long side horizontal to the rollers. This allows you more quilting space before having to advance the quilt. This method works well when you have a large center motif because you can quilt it all at once.

3 For the turquoise outer border, stitch in the ditch along the top border and as far down each side as possible without advancing the quilt. You will continue to stitch in the ditch each time you advance the quilt. Starting at the upper left-hand corner of your quilt, quilt a channel border with ribbon candy (page 40). To do this, quilt a vertical line with your straightedge longarm ruler and then another ¼" (6 mm) from that line. Now space over ½" (1.3 cm) and then echo it ¼" away. Move over 2" (5 cm) and repeat. Fill in the 2" space with ribbon candy. Continue this sequence across the top of the border and down each side as you advance the quilt.

4 In the aqua middle border, mark a grid evenly across. I usually use the border width as my basis for my grid. This border is 5" (12.5 cm) wide after piecing, so mark a grid at about 5" intervals, starting in the middle and working to each side. The spacing doesn't need to be perfect; you may need to fudge it a little. Use the grid to quilt the top and bottom zigzags that will create the peaks and valleys in this design. Quilt the center square between the zigzags, starting at the corner and working toward the zigzags. Stop about ½" (1.3 cm) from the outer zigzag, creating an echo.

5 Fill in the outer triangles of the zigzag with wishbones (page 32). Quilt back-and-forth lines (page 50) in the center of the diamonds.

6 In the gray inner border, quilt ribbon candy and then echo both sides.

7 In the center, work out from the center and quilt the marked circles and scallops. Freehand quilt a star motif in the center circle. Quilt archways (page 43) in the larger space between the circles.

8 Quilt double bubbles (page 37) between the scallop and the largest circle.

9 Finish your scallop with echoed feathers (page 45). Quilt swirls (page 33) around the feathers.

10 Continue to quilt the borders and the center of the quilt as you advance the quilt. Note: You will quilt the turquoise side borders to the edge of the quilt and then quilt the bottom border to create an asymmetrical outer border.

11 Remove the quilt from the frame and trim the edges. Join the binding strips at the ends diagonally to make a continuous binding. Bind the quilt using your favorite method.

Go with the Flow
TABLE RUNNER

FABRICS: Slow and Steady by Tula Pink

This adorable little table runner could be made for all seasons and would make a welcome addition to your table. I made it with a pack of precut charm squares and some background fabric. In addition to the ways I share here, you can mix things up and practice quilting different motifs in the print fabric or fill in the background areas with allover quilting. Either way, it will be stunning.

MATERIALS

24 squares 5" × 5" (12.5 × 12.5 cm) or assorted scraps

⅝ yard (0.5 m) white fabric for background

¼ yard (0.6 m) fabric for binding

¾ yard (0.7 m) fabric for backing

22" × 42" (56 × 106.5 cm) piece of batting

Cutting

CHARM SQUARES

From the 24 squares, cut 72 (J) pieces 1½" × 4½" (3.8 × 11.5 cm). You should be able to cut 3 from each square, which will result in leftover pieces.

BACKGROUND FABRIC

Cut 10 strips 1½" × WOF (width of fabric) (3.8 cm × WOF).

From strips, cut the following:

A: Cut 16 strips 1½" × 1" (3.8 × 2.5 cm).

B: Cut 16 strips 1½" × 1⅜" (3.8 × 3.5 cm).

C: Cut 16 strips 1½" × 1⅞" (3.8 × 4.8 cm).

D: Cut 16 strips 1½" × 2¼" (3.8 × 5.5 cm).

E: Cut 16 strips 1½" × 2¾" (3.8 × 7 cm).

F: Cut 16 strips 1½" × 3⅛" (3.8 × 8 cm).

G: Cut 16 strips 1½" × 3⅝" (3.8 × 9.2 cm).

H: Cut 16 strips 1½" × 4" (3.8 × 10 cm).

I: Cut 8 strips 1½" × 4½" (3.8 × 11.5 cm).

It's helpful to label all of your pieces.

Make Blocks

Use a ¼" (6 mm) seam allowance.

1 Sew the lettered strips together as shown in the diagram (**FIGURE 1**). Press the seams to the background fabric. Sew 16 of the first 4 strips and 8 of the last (IJ) strip.

2 Piece 9 strips together to make 1 block as shown (**FIGURE 2**). Note that some of the fabric strips are rotated 180 degrees from that shown in Step 1. It is very important to have consistent ¼" (6 mm) seams. Press all seams in one direction. Repeat for BlockB except press the seams in the opposite direction (Figure 3). Make 4 of Block A and 4 of Block B, for a total of 8 blocks.

Assembly

1 Lay out your blocks on a table or design wall, placing 2 blocks in each row and alternating A and B blocks starting with Block A (**FIGURE 4**).

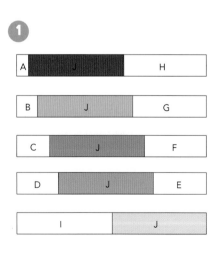

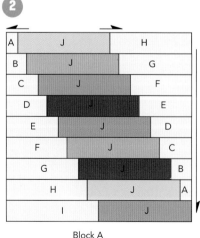

Block A
Make 4.

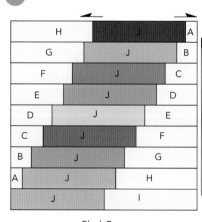

Block B
Make 4.

2 Piece your first row together, pressing the seams to one side.

3 Sew the second row together, pressing the seam in the opposite direction of the first row. Repeat for all 4 rows.

4 Sew 2 rows together, taking care to line up the vertical seams. For best results, pin the seams so they align nicely. Press the seam open to reduce bulk from all the seams coming together (**FIGURE 4**). Repeat for the remaining rows.

Quilting and Finishing

1 For this little table runner, there's no need to mark before loading. Load the table runner with the long side horizontal to the rollers.

2 Quilt free-flowing feathers (page 44) throughout the background areas. For the center feather, quilt small petals on the ends of the feathers and gradually enlarge the petals as you reach the center of the spine, then gradually decrease as you reach the end of the spine.

3 Add back-and-forth lines (page 50) on each side of the feathers to give them dimension Remember to work from left to right.

4 Quilt a ribbon candy motif (page 40) in each of the print strips. Carefully quilt along the edge of 1 strip to get to the next strip. This way, you can quilt all the ribbon candy blocks without starts and stops. As an alternative, you could also quilt wishbones (page 32) or feathers in the print blocks or quilt swirls (page 33) in the background areas. The possibilities are endless.

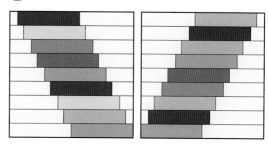
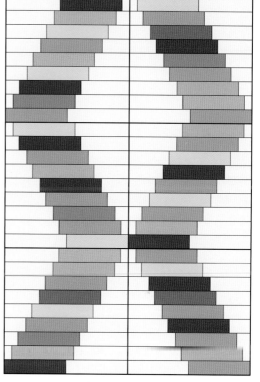

Quilt Assembly

5 Remove the quilt from the frame and trim the edges. Join the binding strips at the ends diagonally to make a continuous binding. Bind the quilt using your favorite method.

CHAPTER 5
GALLERY OF
QUILTS

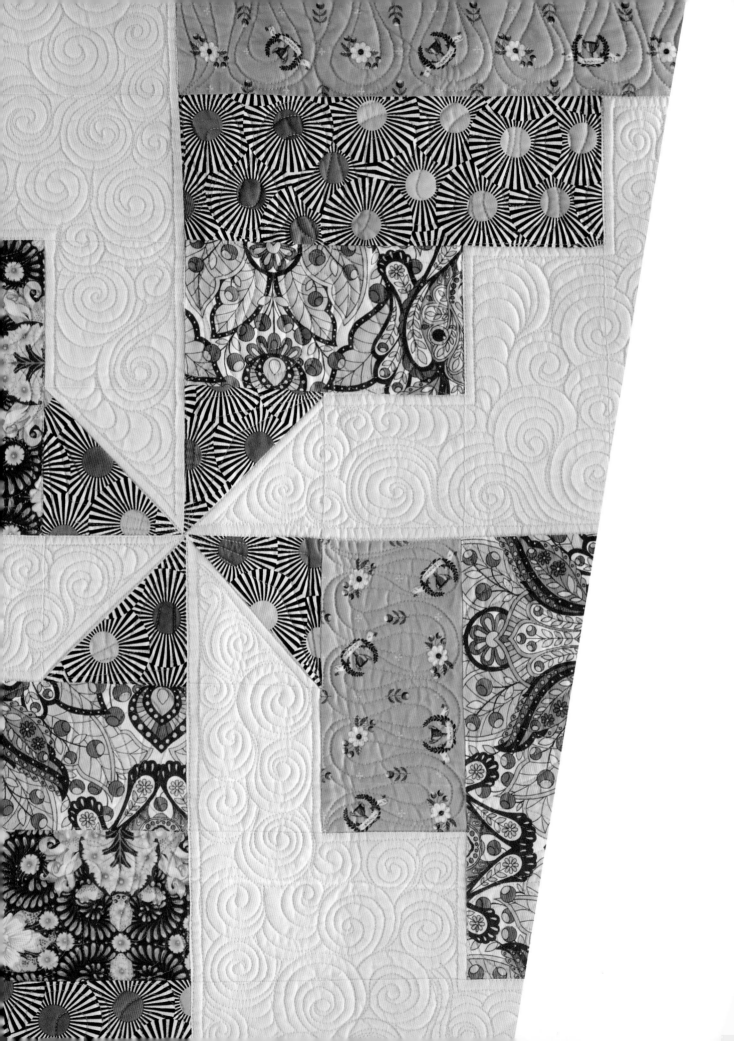

GALLERY OF
QUILTS

Time for a little quilting eye candy! As an aspiring longarm quilter, you are going to love this section of the book. I have put together a compilation of customer quilts, designers' quilts, and my very own quilts that showcase modern longarm quilting designs.

As you study these quilts, look at the design of the overall quilt. Then look at the quilting and consider how the two elements work together. Remember, the goal in most cases is to use the quilting to enhance, not overpower, the quilt design.

FINISHED SIZE: 78″ × 97″ (198 × 246 cm), 2015

Chic and
CHECKERED
QUILT

Made & quilted by **TERESA SILVA**

PATTERN BY: Jenny Pedigo, Helen Robinson, and Sherilyn Mortensen of Sew Kind of Wonderful

FABRICS: Assorted solids by Art Gallery Fabrics

BATTING: Quilters Dream Deluxe Poly

This pattern is by Sew Kind of Wonderful from their book *Contemporary Curved Quilts* (Landauer Publishing, 2014). The designers are all sisters, and together they created their Quick Curve Ruler and have designed many contemporary patterns that use it.

This quilt features very large checkered blocks and large medallion shapes. The quilt was made using all solid fabrics, which allow you to showcase a lot of texture with quilting. I decided to quilt medallions in the gray areas.

I found the center of the gray areas by drawing diagonal lines from each point of the block. Once I had my center, I used circle rulers to draw circles. I started from the center and worked my way out drawing the circle shapes. I used a water-soluble pen to do the marking. Once I had my circles drawn, I went back and did the quilting between the circle lines. I started with a center flower and added archways, triple ribbon candy, and wishbones. For the checkered blocks, I quilted a double continuous line.

FINISHED SIZE: 72" x 72" (183 x 183 cm), 2015

Kwik Ring
AROUND THE HEXIE
QUILT

Made & quilted by **TERESA SILVA**

PATTERN BY: Karie Jewell of Two Kwik Quilters

FABRICS: Assorted fabrics by Tula Pink

BATTING: Quilters Dream Deluxe Poly

This quilt is made up of triangle shapes that form a hexagon in the center. I first drew a large hexagon around the pieced hexagon. The drawn hexagon went to the edge of the quilt on the sides. Next, I stitched in the ditch all the way around the pieced hexagon shape. Then I echoed with a ¼" (6 mm) line. In the area between the drawn hexagon and my echo line, I chose to quilt some paisley feathers with back-and-forth lines to really pop the feathers.

I filled the four corners with simple swirls. For the triangles in the center, I quilted them as diamonds instead of triangles. I started from one point of a triangle and went to the center of the diamond shape about ¼" (6 mm) away from the center. I continued with the line to the other point and up the diamond shape to my start point. I echoed this three times, then filled in with alternating wishbones or pebbles, alternating as I went along.

For the center of the hexagon shape, I created a secondary hexagon design. I again stitched in the ditch on the inside of the pieced blocks and then echoed with a ¼" (6 mm) line. I used the triangle blocks as reference lines to make a ghost hexagon in the center. I just echoed the lines and then filled in the spaces with swirls and pebbles.

FINISHED SIZE: 50" × 60" (127 × 152.5 cm), 2016

114   Longarm Quilting **WORKBOOK**

Ventana
QUILT

Made & quilted by **TERESA SILVA**

PATTERN BY: Nydia Kehnle and Alison Glass

FABRICS: Sun Prints 2016 by Alison Glass

BATTING: Quilters Dream Wool

For this quilt, I echo quilted a ¼" (6 mm) line around the inside and outside edges of all the blocks, and I stitched in the ditch around the blocks. This helped to accent the white areas in the centers between the blocks. I filled in the white areas with simple swirls. On the colored blocks, I quilted an elongated wishbone motif. As you can see, the motifs are very simple but make the quilt look very dramatic.

THREAD TIP

Use a thread color that blends well with all the blocks so you don't have to change your threads as often. This also allows you to quilt an entire row without starting and stopping. In this quilt, I used So Fine 50 thread in white.

Medallion
BABY
QUILT

Made & quilted by **TERESA SILVA**

PATTERN BY: Angela Pingel in *A Quilter's Mixology* (Interweave, a division of F+W Media Inc., 2014)

FABRICS: Into the Deep by Patty Sloniger

BATTING: Quilters Dream Deluxe Poly

This medallion baby quilt had great lines already laid out for me to quilt in. I used the curved piecing to separate the motifs by echoing each curve ¼" (6 mm) from each side to give definition between the pieces. Then I alternated swirls and double bubbles between the sections. For the center, I wanted to showcase the center medallion shape. I found the center and then used my circle rulers and a water-soluble pen to draw lines to create the circles. After the lines were drawn, I quilted the circle shapes freehand. This takes a little practice. If you don't feel you can freehand the circle, you can use a longarm circle ruler and follow the ruler like you would a straightedge ruler. I then went back and added the archways between the lines and a flower in the center. I switched threads with each fabric color change.

FINISHED SIZE: 96" × 97" (244 × 246 cm), 2015

Gravity
QUILT

Made & quilted by **TERESA SILVA**

PATTERN BY: Julie Herman of Jaybird Quilts

FABRICS: Moonshine by Tula Pink

BATTING: Quilters Dream Deluxe Poly

This quilt was a block-of-the-month pattern designed by Julie Herman of Jaybird Quilts. The original quilt that Julie Herman made featured all Kona Cotton solid fabrics. I thought I would try making the quilt in prints. The solid versions of this quilt are pretty amazing, as you can really showcase the quilting, but it was exciting to see how some prints would play out.

This quilt features many different shapes, which I used as my guidelines. Of course, I changed my threads to match the colors nicely.

The outside gray, white, and black diamonds seemed to radiate to me, so I wanted to enhance that with my quilting. I chose to quilt a straight-line border around the diamonds, added a row of pebbles, and finished off with back-and-forth lines in the centers of the diamonds. This design required a lot of stops and starts, which I would not recommend.

I accented each individual block center with a different style of quilting. The center blocks make a great place to experiment with different motifs.

FINISHED SIZE: 72" × 72" (183 × 183 cm), 2016

Friendship
QUILT

Made by **KRISTEN MCVANE**
Quilted by **TERESA SILVA**

PATTERN BY: Kristen McVane

FABRICS: Slow and Steady by Tula Pink

BATTING: Quilters Dream Select Poly

This quilt was made out of friendship. I asked my dear friend Kristen to make me something fabulous for my book because she has a great talent for designing patterns. Thankfully she said she would!

This quilt features awesome spinner blocks. We thought it would be fun to make them look like they were spinning on the quilt. I echo quilted ¼" (6 mm) lines around the print fabrics to set the spinner design apart from the background. Then I quilted the background with lots of swirls to give it nice movement. For the print areas, I quilted a simple triple ribbon candy motif.

MIX IT UP

Mix up your swirls. Use some basic swirls and some swirls with tails to give your quilting movement.

FINISHED SIZE: 56" × 72" (142 × 183 cm), 2016

Trailmix
QUILT

Made by **LESLIE MELTZER**
Quilted by **TERESA SILVA**

PATTERN BY: Julie Herman of Jaybird Quilts

FABRICS: True Colors by Tula Pink

BATTING: Quilters Dream Blend

For this quilt, I again echoed the inside and outside of each of the blocks with a ¼" (6 mm) line to separate the blocks. The quilting in the blocks was easy; I just picked a different motif for each block color. In the purple blocks, I quilted a straight-line motif in the triangle shapes the blocks made with the piecing. In the tangerine blocks, I quilted simple pebbles. And in the green blocks, I quilted basic swirls. I finished with triangles in the white background. This quilt had a lot of texture with all the different motifs. I matched the threads to the fabric colors.

ECHO TIP

Always make sure you are consistent with your quilting. If you are adding an echo with a ¼" (6 mm) line in one area of the quilt, make your echoes in other areas of the quilt the same width.

FINISHED SIZE: 65" × 88" (165 × 223.5 cm), 2015

Sweet Tooth
IN WHITE
QUILT

Made by **LESLIE MELTZER**
Quilted by **TERESA SILVA**

PATTERN BY: Julie Herman of Jaybird Quilts

FABRICS: Blueberry Park by Karen Lewis

BATTING: Quilters Dream Deluxe Poly

This is another fabulous design by Julie Herman of Jaybird Quilts. It was another block-of-the-month pattern that she created using her user-friendly rulers. This quilt features lots of shapes, including hexagons, diamonds, triangles, and half hexagons, that go together so beautifully.

I echo quilted a ¼" (6 mm) line around each block and between the hexagon background and the outer edge to give definition. I quilted the white background area with swirls, and I quilted each block differently.

FINISHED SIZE: 65" × 88" (165 × 223.5 cm), 2016

Sweet Tooth
IN GRAY
QUILT

Made and quilted by **TERESA SILVA**

PATTERN BY: Julie Herman of Jaybird Quilts

FABRICS: Various solid fabrics from my stash

BATTING: Quilters Dream Deluxe Poly

Here is another version of Julie's Sweet Tooth quilt that I pieced with a darker background. I quilted it similar to the one I did for Leslie, but I changed the background filler to a combination of paisleys and clamshells.

KEEP QUILTING

Try to limit the times you actually have to start and stop. The fewer stops you have, the more efficiently you can quilt and the less likely the stitches will come loose.

FINISHED SIZE: 88" × 96" (223.5 × 244 cm), 2016

Space Dust
QUILT

Made and quilted by **TERESA SILVA**

PATTERN BY: Tula Pink

FABRICS: Assorted Tula Pink fabrics from my stash

BATTING: Quilters Dream Deluxe Poly

Tula Pink designed this paper-pieced quilt. This quilt has wonderful negative space in the outer border. It really is a quilter's playground.

I chose this space to do a little doodle quilting. I started by marking areas with my water-soluble marking pen before I loaded my quilt. I randomly made some channels, about 2½" (6.5 cm) wide radiating out from the center and echoed them with a ¼" (6 mm) line. This created a nice space to quilt some ghost flying geese radiating out to the outer edge of the quilt. There really is no rhyme or reason to the doodle quilting except that I consistently quilted arrows all around the quilt. I quilted from the heart, and this is what I ended up with. It was a joy to work on, and I was able to practice all sorts of designs without worrying if they were going to look good or not. In a quilt like this, no one will know if each element is perfect because there is so much going on.

For the center of the quilt, I individually quilted each shape created by the piecing. I followed the line of the shape and then kept echoing the line so that the quilting was about ¼" (6 mm) apart in each block.

FINISHED SIZE : 65" × 65" (165 × 165 cm), 2016

Jellied
LONESTAR
QUILT

Made and quilted by **TERESA SILVA**

PATTERN BY: Terri Ann of Childlike Fascination

FABRICS: Daysail by Bonnie and Camille for Moda Fabrics

BATTING: Quilters Dream Deluxe Poly

This wonderful quilt was made with a jelly roll, which is a selection of precut 2½" × 42" (6.5 × 106.5 cm) fabric strips that are rolled and packaged. A jelly roll is great for making quilts because the fabric is already cut for you. This quilt was challenging for me to piece, but I was very excited with the final outcome—especially after the quilting was done.

Before I loaded this quilt onto my longarm, I marked the diagonal lines to create channels that I later filled with large pearls. I then quilted lines every ½" (1.3 cm) and filled every other line with back-and-forth lines going toward the outside of the quilt. As you can see, I quilted the ½" lines into the border as well. I like how it made the quilt flow together instead of separating the border. This technique works well if you have particularly large borders and want them to look like they haven't just been added to make the quilt larger.

Around the star, I created a big square that appears to be going behind the star. This made a great area to fill in with double bubbles and some archways around the square. For the star, I simply used continuous-line quilting inside each diamond.

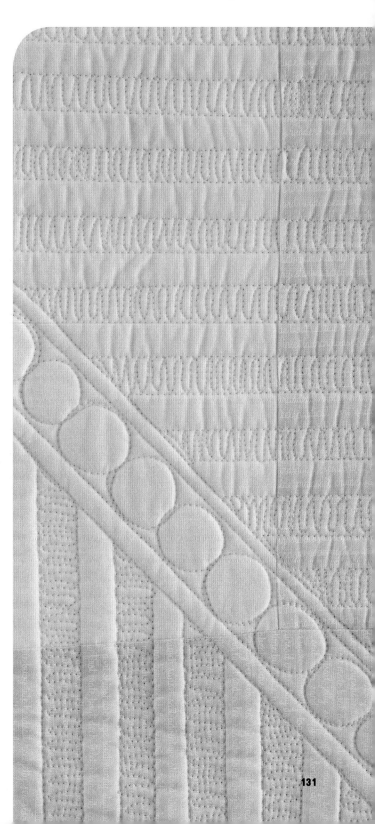

FINISHED SIZE: 90" × 90" (229 × 229 cm), 2016

The Jungle Abstractions:
THE LION
QUILT

Made and quilted by **TERESA SILVA**

PATTERN BY: Violet Craft

FABRICS: Michael Miller Cotton Couture solids

BATTING: Quilters Dream Select Poly

Violet Craft is a master at paper-pieced patterns. I always seem to gravitate toward patterns that I can readily see quilting designs in, especially when I have time to make a quilt of my own.

This was the second lion quilt I made, and what I love about this pattern is all the geometric shapes that create the lion. All of these pieced shapes make an excellent foundation to just follow the lines with straight-line quilting. I used a longarm ruler and took it one shape at a time. The original pattern didn't call for all the extra negative space around the lion. I added it so the lion could fit a queen-size bed and so I could have some negative space in which to quilt.

Before loading the quilt onto my longarm, I drew a couple of the larger star shapes with a water-soluble pen. Marking the shapes beforehand made them much easier to quilt since they were so large. After I had the quilt loaded on my longarm machine, I randomly placed more stars, added more line work around the outside of the design, and created some definition by using back-and-forth lines between those lines. Around the stars, I quilted swirls and swirls with tails mixed with some maze-style background quilting. This gave the quilt a lot of movement around the lion as well and added a lot of interest to the quilting design.

FINISHED SIZE: 74" × 74" (188 × 188 cm), 2016

Persimmon
QUILT

Made and quilted by **TERESA SILVA**

PATTERN BY: Jenny Pedigo, Helen Robinson, and Sherilyn Mortensen of Sew Kind of Wonderful

FABRICS: Moda Bella Solids

BATTING: Quilters Dream Select Poly

Persimmon is a quilt made using the Quick Curve Ruler that the Sew Kind of Wonderful ladies created. They have a huge assortment of patterns and a couple books loaded with tons of inspiration. I chose this pattern from their book *One Wonderful Curve* (Landauer Publishing, 2015) because I'm a huge fan of two-color quilts, especially when I can use solids. Solids show quilting so much better than prints, so it's pretty much a quilter's candy land when you hand me a solid quilt.

For this quilt, I outlined the curved shapes and created a channel all the way around the design using a 1" (2.5 cm) space echoed with ¼" (6 mm) lines on both sides. In the channel, I quilted back-and-forth lines, which really set the blocks away from all the surrounding negative space. This gave me an excellent area to do a lot of freehand swirls, which I think are my favorite motif to quilt. This quilt could have been quilted many ways, including using geometric shapes, such as triangles or squares, or some maze-style background quilting in the negative space. You could create stars or maybe even mirror the curved shapes in the negative space. The possibilities are endless.

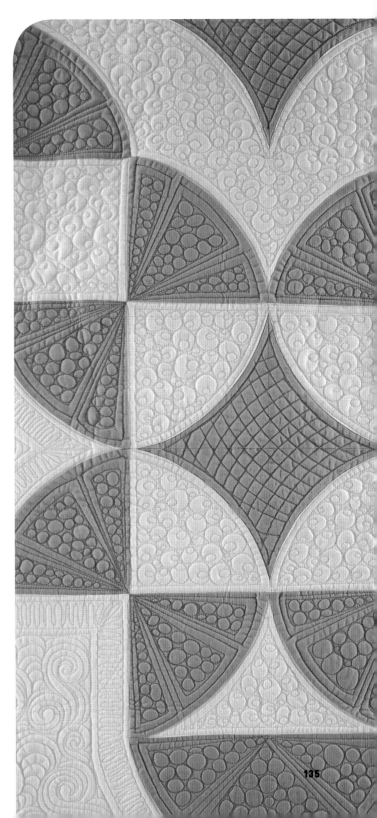

FINISHED SIZE: 60" × 60" (152.5 × 152.5 cm), 2015

136 Longarm Quilting **WORKBOOK**

Glimmer
QUILT

Made and quilted by TERESA SILVA

PATTERN BY: Julie Herman of Jaybird Quilts

FABRICS: Cotton+Steel

BATTING: Quilters Dream Deluxe Poly

I had a lot of fun with the negative space in this quilt. I sectioned off the outside edge by echoing the star shape and making a channel about 2" (5 cm) wide echoed with a ¼" (6 mm) line on both sides. I then filled in this area with pebbles and quilted clamshells to the edge of the quilt. For the blocks themselves, I followed the shapes with straight lines, ribbon candy, and wishbones. I added more pebbles in the center of the quilt.

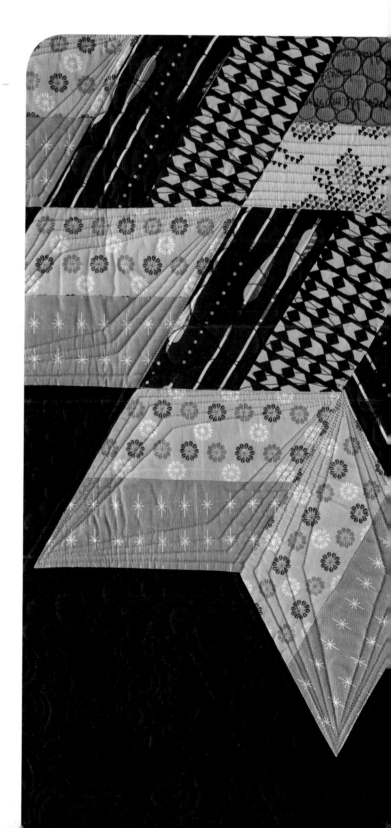

FINISHED SIZE: 64" × 84" (162.5 × 213 cm), 2016

Toes in the Sand
QUILT

Made by **JULIE HERMAN**
Quilted by **TERESA SILVA**

PATTERN BY: Julie Herman of Jaybird Quilts

FABRICS: PB&J by BasicGrey for Moda Fabrics

BATTING: Quilters Dream Select Poly

Toes in the Sand (Jaybird Quilts, 2012) is another block-of-the-month quilt book by Julie Herman. She designed twelve of these amazing geometric blocks that made an excellent playground for quilting. For the blocks, I followed the block shapes and quilted mostly straight lines. For the negative-space triangles, I created a secondary shape in the triangle blocks and broke up the space with swirls, back-and-forth lines, and double bubbles. The partial side borders made a great space to add some maze-style background quilting along with more straight lines.

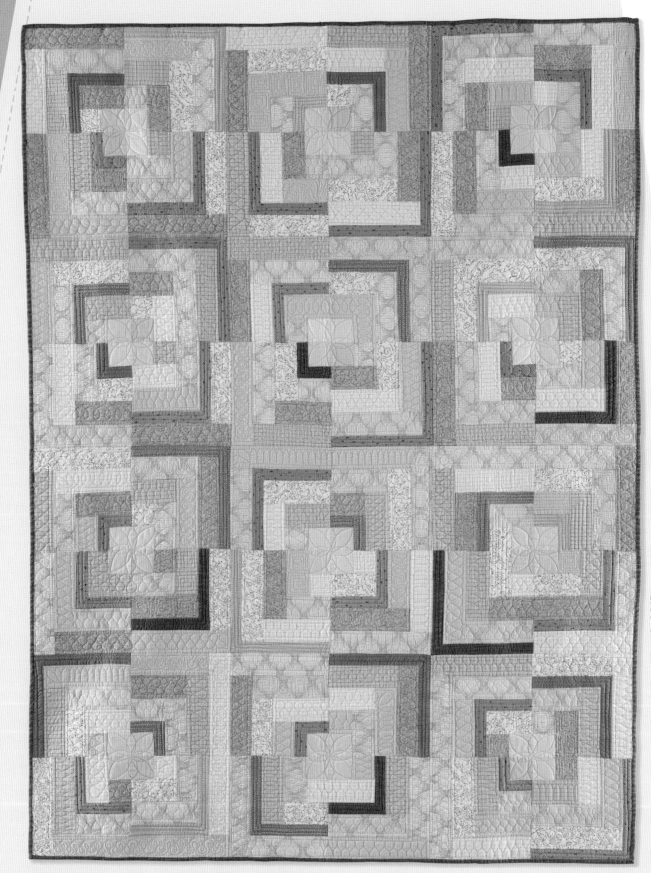

FINISHED SIZE: 60" × 70" (152.5 × 178 cm), 2015

Post & Beam
QUILT

Made by **JANE ST.PIERRE**
Quilted by **TERESA SILVA**

PATTERN BY: Natalie Barnes of Beyond the Reef

FABRICS: Studio Stash III and Studio Stash Yarn Dyes by Jennifer Sampou for Robert Kaufman Fabrics

BATTING: Quilters Dream Select Poly

Natalie Barnes creates some unique modern designs that incorporate lots of fabrics to achieve the look. This quilt is one of my favorites that I've quilted for her. I quilted different designs in all of the strip pieces. It was a fun quilt to work on—no boredom here, as I was able to quilt pretty much every design I could think of. There was no right or wrong to the design; I just quilted whatever I felt like in each strip. I had a great time finishing this quilt!

GO FOR IT!

Don't be afraid to try new quilting motifs on your quilts. This is the best way to learn new motifs or perfect motifs you already know.

Resources

FABRIC

FreeSpirit Fabrics
www.freespiritfabrics.com

Moda Fabrics
www.unitednotions.com

TOOLS

Jaybird Quilts
www.jaybirdquilts.com
Hex N More Ruler; Mini Hex N More Ruler; Sidekick Ruler; Super Sidekick Ruler

The Quilted Pineapple
www.thequiltedpineapple.com
Longarm rulers

Sew Kind of Wonderful
https//sewkindofwonderful.com
Quick Curve Ruler

THREAD

Superior Threads
www.superiorthreads.com
So Fine 50

MARKING TOOLS

Prym Consumer USA
www.dritz.com
Disappearing Ink Marking Pen; Mark-B-Gone Marking Pen

BATTING

Quilters Dream Batting
www.quiltersdreambatting.com

PATTERNS

Beyond the Reef
www.beyondthereef.com

Childlike Fascination
www.childlikefascination.com

Alison Glass
https//alisonglass.com

Jaybird Quilts
www.jaybirdquilts.com

Nydia Kehnle
www.nydiakehnle.com

Kristen McVane
www.stashquilts.com

Angela Pingel
www.angelapingel.com

Tula Pink
wwwtulapink.com

Sew Kind of Wonderful
https//sewkindofwonderful.com

Two Kwik Quilters
www.facebook.com/twokwikquilters

Violet Craft
www.violetcraft.com

Metric Conversion Chart

TO CONVERT	TO	MULTIPLY BY
Inches	Centimeters	2.54
Centimeters	Inches	0.4
Feet	Centimeters	30.5
Centimeters	Feet	0.03
Yards	Meters	0.9
Meters	Yards	1.1

ABOUT THE AUTHOR

Teresa Silva is a self-taught longarm quilter who has been quilting for customers for about six years. She has had the pleasure of quilting for many well-known designers and has had her work featured in books and magazines. Teresa loves sharing her passion for longarm quilting with others and has recently started teaching longarm quilting classes. You can find her work on her website at www.quiltingismybliss.com, and she frequently posts on Instagram, Facebook, and Twitter under the name @quiltingismybliss. Teresa lives in Yakima, Washington, with her patient husband and two sons.

DEDICATION

To my husband, Rick, who believed in me from day one of my longarm journey. Thank you for all of your support and encouragment. It means the world to me!

To our sons, Jacob and Kyler, who roll their eyes and endure conversations about yet another quilt and who give me the most honest feedback. You are always so supportive of my love of quilting.

And finally to my Mom and Dad, who gave me the talents to do what I love every day. I know you are right here with me making my dreams come true!

Acknowledgments

I have so many people who have helped me along my journey that I would love to thank here.

Thank you to Stash (myfabricstash.com) in Walla Walla, Washington, owned by Kristen McVane, Kathy Hamada, and Ann Hamada. These three awesome ladies gave me a chance and let me quilt for them when no one else would. I will be forever grateful for you and your encouragement for me to follow my dreams.

Thank you to United Notions/Moda Fabrics for providing me with fabrics for many of my projects in this book.

Thank you to the ladies of F+W Media who helped me put this book together: Amelia Johanson, Maya Elson, and Stephanie White. I would also like to thank editor Christine Doyle and technical editor ZJ Humbach for their work on this book.

And finally, to my friends who have always encouraged and challenged me to do more. You know who you are!

KEEP EXPANDING YOUR SKILLS WITH THESE GREAT **FONS & PORTER TITLES!**

The Quilter's Paper-Piecing Workbook

Paper Piece with Confidence to Create 18 Gorgeous Quilted Projects

ELIZABETH DACKSON

978-1-63250-181-3
$25.99

Modern Machine Quilting

Make a Perfectly Finished Quilt on Your Home Machine

CATHERINE REDFORD

978-1-4402-4631-9
$24.99

Quilt with Tula & Angela

A Start-to-Finish Guide to Piecing and Quilting Using Color and Shape

TULA PINK AND ANGELA WALTERS

978-1-4402-4545-9
$26.99

Fons&Porter